MARGARET MACMILLAN was the first woman to win the Samuel Johnson Prize for *Peacemakers: The Paris Conference of 1919*. She is the author of numerous books, including *Nixon in China*. She is the warden of St Anthony's College, Oxford.

ALSO BY MARGARET MACMILLAN

Women of the Raj:
the Mothers, Wives, and Daughters of the British Empire in India

Peacemakers: The Paris Conference of 1919 and Its Attempt to End War

Seize the Hour: When Nixon met Mao

THE USES AND ABUSES OF HISTORY

Margaret MacMillan

The Uses and Abuses of History

P

PROFILE BOOKS

First published in Great Britain in 2009 by
PROFILE BOOKS LTD
3A Exmouth House
Pine Street
London EC1R 0JH
www.profilebooks.com

First published in the United States in 2009 by
Random House, Inc., New York
Originally published in Canada in 2008 by
Viking Canada, a division of Penguin Books Ltd

1 3 5 7 9 10 8 6 4 2

Printed and bound in Great Britain by
Clays, Bungay, Suffolk

A CIP catalogue record for this book is available from the British Library.

ISBN 978 1 84668 204 9

FSC
Mixed Sources
Product group from well-managed
forests and other controlled sources
Cert no. SGS-COC-2061
www.fsc.org
© 1996 Forest Stewardship Council

The paper this book is printed on is certified by the © 1996 Forest Stewardship
Council A.C. (FSC). It is ancient-forest friendly. The printer holds FSC chain of
custody SGS-COC-2061

To my nieces and nephews

CONTENTS

Introduction   xi

1. THE HISTORY CRAZE   1
2. HISTORY FOR COMFORT   13
3. WHO OWNS THE PAST?   33
4. HISTORY AND IDENTITY   51
5. HISTORY AND NATIONALISM   79
6. PRESENTING HISTORY'S BILL   91
7. HISTORY WARS   111
8. HISTORY AS A GUIDE   139

Conclusion   165
Acknowledgments   171
Further Reading   177
Index   181

Introduction

History is something we all do, even if, like the man who discovered he was writing prose, we do not always realise it. We want to make sense of our own lives, and often we wonder about our place in our own societies and how we got to be here. So we tell ourselves stories, not always true ones, and we ask questions about ourselves. Such stories and questions inevitably lead us to the past. How did I grow up to be the person I am? Who were my parents? My grandparents? As individuals, we are all, at least in part, products of our own histories, which include our geographical place, our times, our social classes, and our family backgrounds. I am a Canadian who has grown up in Canada, and so I have enjoyed an extraordinary period, unusual in much of the world's history, of peace, stability and prosperity. That has surely shaped the ways in which I look at the world, perhaps with more optimism about things getting better than I might have if I had grown up in Afghanistan or Somalia. And I am also a product of my parents' and grandparents' history. I grew up with some knowledge, incomplete and fragmentary, to be sure, of World War II, which my father fought in, and of World War I, which drew in both my grandfathers.

We use history to understand ourselves, and we ought to use it to understand others. If we find out that an acquaintance has suffered a catastrophe, that knowledge helps us to avoid causing him pain. (If we find that he has enjoyed great good luck, that may affect how we treat him in another way!) We can never assume that we are all the same, and that is as true in business and politics as it is in personal relations. How can we Canadians understand the often passionate feelings of French nationalists in Quebec if we do not know something about the past that has shaped and continues to shape them, the memories of the conquest by the British in 1759 and the sense that French-speakers had become second-class citizens? Or the mixture of resentment and pride that so many Scots feel toward England now that Scotland has struck oil? If we know nothing of what the loss of the Civil War and Reconstruction meant to Southern whites, how can we understand their resentment toward Yankees that has lingered into the present day? Without knowing the history of slavery and the discrimination and frequent violence that blacks suffered even after emancipation, we cannot begin to grasp the complexities of the relationship between the races in the United States. In international affairs, how can we understand the deep hostility between Palestinians and Israelis without knowing something of their tragic conflicts?

History is bunk, Henry Ford famously said, and it is sometimes hard for us, perhaps especially in North America, to recognise that history is not a dead subject. It does not lie there safely in the past for us to look at when the mood takes us. History can be helpful; it can also be very dangerous. It is wiser to think of history not as a pile of dead leaves or a collection of dusty artefacts but as a pool, sometimes benign, often sulfurous, that lies under the present, silently shaping our institutions, our ways of thought, our likes and dislikes. We call on it, even in North America, for validation and for lessons and advice. Validation, whether of group identities, for demands, or for justification, almost always comes from using the past. You feel your life has a meaning if you are part of a much larger group, which predated your existence and which will survive you (carrying, however, some of your essence into the future). Sometimes we abuse history, creating one-sided or false histories to justify treating others badly, seizing their land, for example, or killing them. There are also many lessons and much advice offered by history, and it is easy to pick and choose what you want. The past can be used for almost anything you want to do in the present. We abuse it when we create lies about the past or write histories that show only one perspective. We can draw our lessons carefully or badly. That does not mean we should not look to history for understanding, support and help; it does mean that we should do so with care.

1

THE HISTORY CRAZE

History, and not necessarily the sort that professional historians are doing, is widely popular these days, even in North America, where we have tended to look toward the future rather than the past. It can be partly explained by market forces. People are better educated and, particularly in the mature economies, have more leisure time and are retiring from work earlier. Not everyone wants to retire to a compound in the sun and ride adult tricycles for amusement. History can be helpful in making sense of the world we live in. It can also be fascinating, even fun. How can even the best novelist or playwright invent someone like Augustus Caesar or Catherine the Great, Galileo or Florence Nightingale? How can screenwriters create better action stories or human dramas than exist, thousand upon thousand, throughout the many centuries of recorded history? There is a thirst out there both for knowledge and to be entertained, and the market has responded with enthusiasm.

Museums and art galleries mount huge shows around historical characters like Peter the Great or on specific periods in history. Around the world, new museums open every year to commemorate moments, often grim ones, from the past. China has museums devoted to Japanese atrocities committed during World War II. Washington, Jerusalem, and Montreal have Holocaust museums. Television has channels devoted entirely to history (often, it must be said, showing a past that seems to be made up largely of battles and the biographies of generals); historic sites are wilting under the tramp of tourists; history movies – think of all the recent ones on Queen Elizabeth I alone – are making money; and the proliferation of popular histories shows that publishers have a good idea of where profits are to be made. Ken Burns's documentaries, from the classic Civil War series to his one on World War II, are aired repeatedly. In Canada, Mark Starowicz's *People's History* drew millions of viewers. The *Historica Minutes* produced by the private foundation Historica, devoted to promoting Canadian history, are so popular among Canadian teenagers that they often do school projects where they make their own minutes. In the United Kingdom, David Starkey's series on British monarchs have made him rich and as famous as the kings and queens themselves.

Many governments now have special departments devoted to commemorating the past – or, as it is often grandly designated, "heritage." In Canada, the Department of Canadian Heritage exhorts Canadians to learn about Canada's history, culture, and land: "Heritage is our collective treasure, given to us and ours to bequeath to our children." The term can encompass virtually anything: language, folk dances, recipes, antiques, paintings, customs, buildings. There are societies to celebrate antique cars or guns, baseball cards or matchboxes. In England, a young architect has founded the Chimneypot Preservation and Protection Society to save, as its mission decrees, "the Sentinels of Time".

France, which has had a particularly active Ministry of Culture for decades, declared 1980 the Année du Patrimoine. Locals dressed up to reenact the great moments of their history. In the following years, the number of heritage sites and monuments on the official list doubled. Scores of new museums – devoted to the wooden shoe, for example, or the chestnut forest – appeared. At the end of the decade, the government set up a special commission to oversee the commemoration of the two-hundredth anniversary of the French Revolution in 1989.

In France there has been an explosion of reenactments of the past, festivals, and special months, weeks, and days. The possibilities, of course, are endless: the starts and ends of wars, the births and deaths of famous people, the first publication of a book or the first performance of an opera, a strike, a demonstration, a trial, a revolution, even natural disasters. And the activity is not all government inspired; much comes from local and volunteer initiatives. Châlons-sur-Marne recognised the centenary of the invention of canning. It is not just in France that communities want to revisit their past: Perth, Ontario, had a week of festivities in 1993 to celebrate the giant cheese that it sent to the World's Fair in Chicago in 1893. As enterprising local governments and businesses have realised, the past is also good for tourism.

Governments tend to assume that proper attention and care of the past will do the present good. In the United States, the National Historic Preservation Act assumes that a sense of the past will help make good Americans. The nation's heritage must be preserved, it says, "in order to give a sense of orientation to the American people". President George W. Bush's executive order of 2003 entitled "Preserve America" echoed that sentiment: "The Federal Government shall recognise and manage the historic properties in its ownership as assets that can support department and agency missions while contributing to the vitality and economic well-being of the Nation's communities and fostering a broader appreciation for the development of the United States and its underlying values."

The passion for the past is clearly about more than market forces or government policies. History responds to a variety of needs, from greater understanding of ourselves and our world to answers about what to do. For many human beings, an interest in the past starts with themselves. That is in part a result of biology. Like other creatures, humans have a beginning and an ending, and in between lies their story. It probably also has to do with the realisation that today the great majority of people live in a rapidly changing world where long-standing relationships that were once taken for granted – whether with places or with people such as family or friends – no longer exist for many. Part of the current fascination with preserving heritage comes from the fear that we are losing priceless and irreplaceable pieces of the past, whether they are dying languages or decaying buildings. Sometimes the preservationists seem to want time itself to stand still. In New York, to take a current debate, should the tenements of the Lower East Side be replaced by modern, more salubrious buildings? Or should they be kept, as a spokeswoman for the Tenement Museum said, "to remind us of the experience lived and worked inside them"?

Nineteen million people around the world are now signed up to the online Friends Reunited, which will put you in touch with long-lost friends from the distant past, even from your earliest school days. If anyone wants to go still further back, and an increasing number of people do, he or she can research genealogies. It is understandable, said a spokesman for the College of Arms in London, "in a throwaway society where everything is ephemeral". Most national archives now have special sections set aside for patrons who are investigating their family histories.

Thanks to the Mormons, who collect parish registers, genealogies, and birth records for their own purposes, Salt Lake City houses an enormous worldwide collection of records. The Internet has made it even easier, with dozens of sites where you can search for your ancestors, with more specialised ones dedicated to a single family name. In Canada and the United Kingdom, the popular television show *Who Do You Think You Are?* caters to our fascination with celebrities and the hunt for ancestors as it traces back, often with surprising results, the family trees of the famous.

Recent developments in science make it possible to go beyond the printed records. The decoding of DNA means that scientists can now trace an individual's ancestry back through the mother's line and can find others with the same genetic makeup. As the databases of information build up, it becomes increasingly possible to see how human beings have migrated over the years. This is important for anyone who wants to go back beyond where the paper trail peters out. It is particularly important for those who never had much of a paper trail to begin with. Those immigrants who came in great waves to the New World in the nineteenth and twentieth centuries to escape a miserable and uncertain life in Europe often lost all links with their pasts, sometimes indeed even their old names. For the descendants of American slaves, who lacked even the faintest hope of recovering the path their ancestors followed from Africa and not much more chance of finding out what happened to them once they were in the United States, DNA has suddenly opened the door to self-knowledge. A moving program called *African American Lives,* which was broadcast by PBS in 2006, looked at the DNA of famous black Americans, Oprah Winfrey and Quincy Jones among them. Sometimes the results are disappointing: family stories about the great-grandparent who was descended from kings are often just that – stories. Sometimes there are surprises, as when an obscure professor of accounting in Florida found he was descended from Genghis Khan. Perhaps, thought the professor, he owed his administrative skills to his terrifying ancestor.

The current fascination for people's personal histories can be narcissistic – how much time should human beings spend gazing at themselves, after all? – but it also comes from the desire to know more about what made people who they are and what made the world in which they happen to live. If people can stand back and see their own histories in a wider perspective, then they can see how they are the products not just of particular individuals but of whole societies and cultures. Members of certain ethnic groups may find that they have inherited views on other ethnic groups, and may also find that others regard them in particular ways. History has shaped humans' values, their fears, their aspirations, their loves and their hatreds. When we start to realise that, we begin to understand something of the power of the past.

Even when people think they are striking out in new directions, their models often come from the past. How often have we seen revolutionaries, committed to building new worlds, slip back unconsciously into the habits and ways of those they have replaced? Napoleon came to power as the result of the French Revolution, but the court he set up was modelled on that of the displaced Bourbons. The top Soviet Communists lived within the walls of the Kremlin, as the czars had once done. Stalin looked back to Ivan the Terrible and Peter the Great as his predecessors, as, I suspect, Vladimir Putin did when he was president. The Chinese Communists scorned China's traditional society, but their top leaders chose to live right at the heart of Beijing, where the imperial court had once been. Mao Zedong himself withdrew into mysterious seclusion, much as the emperors had done over the centuries.

"Men make their own history," said Karl Marx, "but they do

not make it as they please: they do not make it under self-selected circumstances, but under circumstances existing already, given and transmitted from the past."

During the Cold War, though, history appeared to have lost much of its old power. The world that came into being after 1945 was divided up between two great alliance systems and two competing ideologies, both of which claimed to represent the future of humanity. American liberal capitalism and Soviet-style Communism were about, so they said, building new societies, perhaps even new human beings. The old conflicts, between Serbs and Croats, Germans and French, or Christians and Muslims, were just that and were consigned, in Leon Trotsky's memorable phrase, to the dustbin of history. The threat of massive nuclear war, of course, was always present, and from time to time, during the Cuban missile crisis in 1962, it looked as if the last moment of the planet had come. But it did not, and in the end most of us simply forgot about the danger. Nuclear weapons took on a benign aspect: after all, the balance of terror meant that neither superpower dared attack the other without risking its own destruction. People at the time assumed that the United States and the Soviet Union would remain locked in their conflict, between war and peace, perhaps forever. In the meantime, the developed world enjoyed unparalleled prosperity, and new economic powers, many in Asia, appeared on the scene.

My students used to tell me how lucky I was to be teaching history. Once you have got a period or the events of a war straight, so they assumed, you don't have to think about them again. It must be so nice, they would say, not to redo your lecture notes. The past, after all, is the past. It cannot be changed. History, they seemed to say, is no more demanding than digging a stone out of the ground. It can be fun to do but is not really necessary. What does it matter what happened then? This is now.

When the Cold War abruptly ended in 1989 with the collapse

of the Soviet Empire in Europe, the world enjoyed a brief, much too brief, period of optimism. Collectively, it failed to recognise that the certainties of the post-1945 years had been replaced by a more complicated international order. Instead, most people assumed that as the remaining superpower, the United States would surely become a benevolent hegemon. Societies would benefit from a "peace dividend" because there would be no more need to spend huge amounts on the military. Liberal democracy had triumphed and Marxism itself had gone into the dustbin. History, as Francis Fukuyama put it, had come to an end, and a contented, prosperous and peaceful world was moving into the next millennium.

In fact, many of the old conflicts and tensions remained, frozen into place just under the surface of the Cold War. The end of that great struggle brought a thaw, and long-suppressed dreams and hatreds bubbled to the surface again. Saddam Hussein's Iraq invaded Kuwait, basing its claims on dubious history. We discovered that it mattered that Serbs and Croats had many historical reasons to fear and hate each other, and that there were peoples within the Soviet Union who had their own proud histories and who wanted their independence. Many of us had to learn who the Serbs and Croats were and where Armenia or Georgia lay on the map. In the words of the title of Misha Glenny's book on central Europe, we witnessed the rebirth of history. Of course, as so often happens, some people went too far the other way and blamed everything that was going wrong in the Balkans in the 1990s, to take one of the most egregious cases, on "age-old hatreds," which conveniently overlooked the wickedness of Slobodan Milošević, then the president, and his ilk, who were doing their best to destroy Yugoslavia and dismember Bosnia. Such an attitude allowed outside powers to stand by wringing their hands helplessly for far too long.

The last two decades have been troubled and bewildering ones, and, not surprisingly, many people have turned to history to try to understand what is going on. Books on the history of the Balkans sold well as Yugoslavia fell to pieces. Today, publishers are rushing to commission histories of Iraq or to reissue older works. T. E. Lawrence's *Seven Pillars of Wisdom*, which describes the Arab struggle against Turkey for independence, is a bestseller again, and particularly popular with American soldiers serving in Iraq. My own book on the Paris Peace Conference of 1919, where so much of the foundation of the modern world was laid, could not find a publisher in the 1980s. As one publisher said, no one wanted to read about a bunch of dead white men sitting around talking about long-forgotten peace settlements. By the 1990s, the subject had come to seem a lot more relevant.

Today's world is far removed from the stasis of the Cold War. It looks more like that of the decade before 1914 and the outbreak of World War I or the world of the 1920s. In those days, as the British Empire started to weaken and other powers, from Germany to Japan to the United States, challenged it for hegemony, the international system became unstable. Today, the United States still towers over the other powers but not as much as it once did. It has been badly damaged by its involvement in Iraq, and it faces challenges from the rising Asian powers of China and India and its old rival Russia. Economic troubles bring, as they brought in the past, domestic pressures for protection and trade barriers. Ideologies – then Fascism and Communism, now religious fundamentalisms – challenge the assumptions of liberal internationalism and wage war on powers they see standing in their way. And the world still has, as it had in the first half of the twentieth century, the unreasoning forces of ethnic nationalism.

2

HISTORY FOR
COMFORT

Dealing with uncertainty is not easy, and it is not surprising that we seize on whatever might help us – including history. The uses and abuses of history in decision-making are something I will come to later, but for the present I want to look at why history can be at once so reassuring and so appealing.

To begin with, it can offer simplicity when the present seems bewildering and chaotic.

Over the years, historians have tried to discern grand patterns, perhaps one grand pattern, that explain everything. For some religions, history provides evidence of the working out of a divine purpose. For the German philosopher Georg Wilhelm Friedrich Hegel, it demonstrated the working out of the infinite spirit (*Geist*) on earth. Karl Marx built on Hegel to produce his "scientific" history, which purported to show that history was moving inexorably toward its destined end of full Communism. To Johann Gottfried Herder, the influential German thinker of the late eighteenth century, history showed that an organic German nation had existed for centuries, although in political terms it had not yet reached its full potential. For imperialists like Sir

Charles Dilke, the study of the past confirmed the superiority of the British race. Arnold Toynbee, whose work is largely neglected now, saw a pattern of challenge and response as civilisations grew great in overcoming obstacles and then failed as they turned soft and lazy. The Chinese, unlike most Western thinkers, did not see history as a linear process at all. Their scholars talked in terms of a dynastic cycle where dynasties came and went in an unending repetition, following the unchanging pattern of birth, maturity and death all under the aegis of heaven.

History, and perhaps that is the case today, can also be an escape from the present. When the world is complicated and changing rapidly, not necessarily for the better, it is no surprise that we look back to what we mistakenly think was a simpler and clearer world. Conservatives dream of small towns painted by Norman Rockwell, where children played innocently in their gardens with no grown-up predators to disturb them, where men and women were comfortable in their roles, and where the sun shone on day after day of happiness. In Canada, an artist with the improbable name of Trisha Romance sells thousands upon thousands of prints of children in pinafores and sailor suits. The period is vaguely Victorian: horses draw carriages and sleighs, candles twinkle on Christmas trees, and families nestle around roaring fires. No one is ever sad or hungry or ragged in her past. Leftists for their part hark back to the glory days when the union movement was strong and the bosses were on the run. Behind much of the current fascination with World War II lies the feeling, certainly on the Allied side, that it was the last morally unambiguous good war. German Nazis, Italian Fascists, and Japanese militarists were so clearly bad people who had to be defeated. (The fact that we were allied with one of the greatest tyrants of the twentieth century in Joseph Stalin is something to be overlooked.) The wars since have not been as clear-cut. The

Korean War, true, was necessary to defeat Soviet expansionism, but General Douglas MacArthur's attempt to turn it into a crusade against Chinese Communism divided Americans among themselves and against their allies. Vietnam was a catastrophe for the United States, and now the occupation of Iraq is looking like another.

We are also short of heroes today – or too aware of our leaders' shortcomings – which may help to explain the cult of Winston Churchill, a cult that is perhaps even more pronounced in North America than it is in the United Kingdom. The British, after all, have had direct experience of Churchill in other roles than that of the great World War II leader. They are more likely to remember his long political career with its share of mistakes and failures. In North America, the Churchill who is remembered is largely the towering figure who fought on alone against the Axis and who helped craft the Allied victory, not the author of the disastrous Gallipoli landings in World War I or the ailing prime minister who stayed too long in office in the 1950s. President George W. Bush is, not surprisingly, fond of comparing himself to the first Churchill, not the second.

Political leaders have always known the value of comparing themselves to great figures from the past. It helps to give them stature and legitimacy as the heirs to the nation's traditions. In comparing himself to Ivan the Terrible and Peter the Great, Stalin was taking on their mantle as builders of a greater Russia. Saddam Hussein in turn compared himself to Stalin or, drawing on the Islamic and Iraqi past, to Saladin. The last shah of Iran tried to draw a line down through the centuries from Cyrus and Darius to his own dynasty. Mao Zedong liked to point to the parallels between himself and the Qin emperor who created China in 221 B.C.

Our present longing for heroes is more than political

expediency. We are anxious to get the testimony of our war veterans before they die, for example, because we feel they have lessons to teach us. And we worry about how to commemorate them properly. As the last, very old veterans of World War I are dying off, a number of countries have considered holding a state funeral, usually given only for heads of state or extraordinary figures like Churchill himself, for the last soldier to die. The discussions have been macabre, about, for example, how to determine who is really the last. Do veterans who have lived all their lives in other countries count? What if a government gives a funeral and then another veteran is discovered? In 2006, in France, two more ancient veterans appeared out of obscurity.

The veterans themselves and their families have shown little enthusiasm for the pomp and circumstance. When the then president of France, Jacques Chirac, announced in 2005 that the last veteran would be buried in a special spot, perhaps the Pantheon itself, he had a cool response. Lazare Ponticelli, one of France's last World War I veterans, said firmly, "If I turn out to be the last survivor, I say no. It would be an insult to all those who died before me and were not given any honors at all". He wanted, and got, a simple memorial service because, he said, he did not think the nation's attention should be directed at one person when so many hundreds of thousands suffered and died. Chirac hastily backtracked, and his government talked in vague terms about making any obsequies an occasion to symbolise European reconciliation.

In Canada, the Dominion Institute, which has shown great entrepreneurial talent for making Canadians feel guilty about how little they know about their own past, launched a petition to give the last Canadian veteran a state funeral. The government, which was initially noncommittal, bowed in the face of what looked like a groundswell of public opinion and allowed a vote in the House

L178, 689

of Commons. Not surprisingly, no member dared vote no on such an emotive issue. Again, the families of the veterans themselves were unenthusiastic. What also made it awkward was that one of the two surviving Canadian veterans at the time of the vote, John Babcock, a lively old man who told interviewers about his attempts to lose his virginity during the war, had lived in the United States since the early 1920s.

Often the desire to hold a state funeral reflects the concerns of the living. The British Conservative leader, Iain Duncan Smith, argued, with one eye on the voters, that it would be a way of commemorating the whole generation that was there at the start of "the century of the common man." When the Italian government buried the last Italian veteran with full state honours, the president, Carlo Azeglio Ciampi, described the commemoration as "living and precious testimony to the sacrifice of the boys who fought . . . to make our country great, free, and united". In Canada, Rudyard Griffiths, head of the Dominion Institute, said, "If there ever was a time for Canada and Canadians to be bold and generous in commemoration of our history, in commemoration of our shared values, surely the passing of the last Great War veteran is that moment".

We call on the past to help us with our values at least in part because we no longer trust the authorities of today. We suspect our politicians of being self-seeking place holders. Too many heads of companies have turned out to be cooking the books or giving themselves lavish emoluments. The craze for gossip fills the pages of *Hello!* magazine or *Vanity Fair,* but it also leaves us with the uneasy sense that there are no good and honest people left. We know too much, whether it is about President Bill Clinton's sex life or Britney Spears's drug problems. We read of doctors making mistakes or schoolteachers telling lies. All this happened in the past, of course, but not under the intense spotlights that the media and the Internet provide today. History comforts us, even though, paradoxically, we know less and less about it.

In a secular world, which is what most of us in Europe and North America live in, history takes on the role of showing us good and evil, virtues and vices. Religion no longer plays as important a part as it once did in setting moral standards and transmitting values. Congregations at the old mainstream churches have declined sharply. It is true that there are huge evangelical churches out there, but they are as much about entertainment and socialising as religion. The millions who describe themselves as born-again Christians often have, according to surveys, the sketchiest of ideas about what it is they are adhering to. And even those who continue to have faith in a divine being may wonder how he or she can allow such evils as the twentieth century witnessed. History with a capital *H* is being called in to fill the void. It restores a sense not necessarily of a divine being but of something above and beyond human beings. It is our authority: it can vindicate us and judge us, and damn those who oppose us.

President Bush has, according to news stories, been reading a lot of history lately, and in it he apparently found some comfort as his presidency stumbled toward its end and he sank ever lower in the opinion polls. He has taken to comparing himself to President Harry Truman, the untried vice president who found himself in office when President Franklin Delano Roosevelt died in 1945. Truman, who came to office singularly ill prepared, thanks to FDR's propensity to keep important matters to himself, was frequently written off at the time as the haberdasher from Missouri. During his tenure, his ratings were often as low as Bush's are today. "To err is Truman", said one wit.

History has been kinder, and Truman is now generally rated by historians and pundits as one of the better American presidents of the twentieth century. He found himself facing an increasingly belligerent Soviet Union and a deteriorating situation on the ground in Europe and met the challenge head-on. He and his administration made the decisions that laid the groundwork for the United States' confrontation of the Soviet Union during the long Cold War. They adopted policies including the Marshall Plan, unprecedented peacetime defence measures, and the establishment of NATO, all of which probably saved Western Europe from Soviet domination. Moreover, Truman showed by his actions that the United States was prepared to contain the spread of Soviet influence. In 1948–49, the United States led the West in circumventing the Soviet blockade of the western zone in Berlin through a massive airlift. The next year Truman sent American forces to Korea to beat back the attack from the Communist North on the South. The Truman administration, many would argue even today, made possible the long confrontation with the Soviet bloc and, ultimately, the triumph of the West in 1989.

In the 2004 election campaign, Bush referred repeatedly and with admiration to Truman. As Bush grew more unpopular, the references to Truman grew more frequent. In December 2006 he told congressional leaders that although Truman had not been popular at the time, history had shown that he was right. In another comparison to the Cold War, Bush has talked often about the struggle with terrorism and fundamentalist Islam as one that will last for generations. In a speech to the graduating class at West Point in May 2006, he compared himself, implicitly, to Truman, who, he said, did what was right even though he was often criticised at the time: "By the actions he took, the institutions he built, the alliances he forged and the doctrines he set down, President Truman laid the foundations for America's victory in the Cold War." Bush did not mention the rather awkward fact that

Truman was a Democrat. Nor did he refer to another significant point of difference: Truman worked through the United Nations rather than treating it with contempt. The differences were not missed by the press or the Democrats, but the White House tried to spin such inconvenient details away. Press secretary Tony Snow denied that Bush was comparing himself to Truman; rather, he was reminding Americans that as in the Cold War, they faced an enemy motivated by ideology and global ambitions whose defeat would take a long time.

If history is the judge to which we appeal, then it can also find against us. It can highlight our mistakes by reminding us of those who, at other times, faced similar problems but who made different, perhaps better decisions. President Bush refused to deal with Iran, even though it has huge influence in the Middle East and in particular in Iraq. His critics remembered when another American president faced a situation where the United States was bogged down in an unwinnable war and was losing much of its authority in the world. President Richard Nixon decided that he had to get the United States out of Vietnam and rebuild American prestige, and that the key to doing both lay in Beijing. Even though the United States and the People's Republic were bitter enemies that had had virtually no contact with each other for decades, he boldly embarked on an initiative to bring about mutual recognition and, so he hoped, mutual help. When I was lecturing in the United States about *Nixon and Mao,* my book on the president's 1972 trip to China, a question I was asked repeatedly was, if Nixon were president today, would he be going to Tehran for help in getting the United States out of Iraq?

As a judge, history also undermines the claims of leaders to omniscience. Dictators, perhaps because they know their own lies so well, have usually realised the power of history. Consequently, they have tried to rewrite, deny, or destroy the past.

Robespierre in revolutionary France and Pol Pot in 1970s Cambodia each set out to start society from the beginning again. Robespierre's new calendar and Pol Pot's Year Zero were designed to erase the past and its suggestions that there were alternative ways of organising society. The founder of China, the Qin emperor, reportedly destroyed all the earlier histories, buried the scholars who might remember them, and wrote his own history. Successive dynasties were not as brutal, but they, too, wrote their own histories of China's past. Mao went one better: he tried to destroy all memories and all artefacts that, by reminding the Chinese people of the past, might prevent him from remodelling them into the new Communist men and women. With his encouragement, young Red Guards stampeded through China, smashing priceless porcelain, burning books, tearing down temples and statues, and beating up and frequently killing teachers, writers, priests, anyone who could be accused of transmitting the old. The Forbidden City in Beijing was only saved because Zhou Enlai sent soldiers to protect it. In the Soviet Union, Stalin wrote his great rival Leon Trotsky out of the books and the photographs and the records until Trotsky became, in George Orwell's chilling formulation, "an un-person." The true record of Trotsky showed, after all, that Stalin was not the natural heir to Lenin, the revered founder of the Soviet Union, and that he had not played the crucial role in the victory of the Bolsheviks over their many enemies.

Their attitude toward history did not, of course, stop the great dictators from trying to ensure their own immortality through statues, monuments, tombs and, in later days, photographs and films. Stalin wrote his own history of Communism in the Soviet Union, in which the only two individuals who figure in its triumphant progress are himself and Lenin. They struggle against various enemies, none of whom are named. The Qin emperor built a massive tomb that was meant to last through eternity. (In Mecca, the Saudi religious and political authorities are trying to enshrine Muhammad in a different way, by taking him out of history so that he is no longer human at all. Religious police warn pilgrims off from praying at sites, such as the cave where the Prophet is said to have received the first message from God, on the grounds that such prayer is idolatry. Over the past half century, the buildings that housed the Prophet and his family have one by one been destroyed, down to their foundations. In the past two decades alone, according to the Gulf Institute, 95 per cent of the oldest buildings in Mecca, dating back more than a thousand years, have vanished.)

Our faith in history frequently spills over into wanting to set the past to rights through apologies and compensation for past actions. Now, there is a good case to be made for individuals and organisations admitting that they have done wrong and offering some form of redress. The Swiss banks that made profits from wealth confiscated from Jews were benefiting from and condoning the crimes of the Nazis and ought to have paid compensation to the heirs of those who suffered. The German state rightly paid compensation over the years to the families of the Jews killed by Adolf Hitler's regime. The Canadian and American governments certainly had an obligation to pay back the Japanese whose property was illegitimately seized when they were rounded up and interned during World War II. The internments themselves of those Japanese who were citizens was of dubious legality. Both governments have apologised and paid compensation to all survivors. In all those cases, the link between those who were sinned against and those who did the sinning was direct and clear.

Often the link is less clear, but the apology makes political sense in the present. Queen Elizabeth's apologies to the Maori of New Zealand for the illegal seizure of their land in the nineteenth century did not mean that she was accepting blame; rather, New Zealand society and the New Zealand government were moving toward settling outstanding issues with the Maori and trying to redress the disadvantages they had suffered. In 2004, three American senators introduced a bill for an official apology to all Native peoples for the "long history of official depredations and ill-conceived policies by the United States." Cynics noted that in an election year, the bill's sponsors may have been moved by the fact that the Native vote was key in several states. The bill ultimately failed to pass.

The acceptance of responsibility and the act of repentance can be healthy for societies struggling to deal with past horrors. In South Africa, with the ending of apartheid, public figures, both black and white, began to talk about how to move on without allowing the past to tear society apart. At the end of the 1980s, as President Frederik Willem de Klerk and his white Nationalist Party negotiated the end of apartheid with Nelson Mandela and the African National Congress, their common challenge was to ensure a peaceful transition to black majority rule. The difficulty was both to reassure the former oppressors – the police and security forces, for example – that they would not be punished for obeying orders and to appease the understandable longing for revenge and retribution of the blacks whom they had oppressed. The deal, and it was a difficult one to make, was that a commission to examine the past would have the power to grant amnesty to its witnesses and to make recommendations about reparations to the victims of apartheid. In 1995, less than two years after the first multiracial elections, the South African parliament passed the Promotion of National Unity and Reconciliation Act. The Truth and Reconciliation Commission started hearings in the spring of 1996 and produced its final report two years later. It was an extraordinary and moving experience which brought the evils of apartheid into the open. The commission held 140 hearings, in all parts of South Africa, and collected some twenty-two thousand statements from the victims of apartheid. Seven thousand members of the old regime applied for amnesties. Former secret policemen came forward to admit torture and killing. Black witnesses wept and prayed as they relived what had happened to them and their families. Of course the commission did not heal all wounds. The granting of amnesties remains unpopular especially with blacks, and the payment of reparations has been fitful and slow. Nevertheless, by the time the commission finished its hearings in 1998, South Africans of all colors and classes had examined and dealt with the record of apartheid and begun to move forward into a shared future.

Is it healthy, though, for societies to apologise for things that were done in different centuries and under different sets of beliefs? Politicians and others have been quick to make all sorts of apologies, even when it is difficult to see why they need feel any responsibility – or what good an apology would do. The pope apologised for the Crusades. The daughter of the British poet John Betjeman apologised to a town near London for a line in one of his poems which read, "Come friendly bombs and fall on Slough / It isn't fit for humans now". In the 1990s, President Bill Clinton apologised for slavery and Tony Blair for the Irish potato famine. A descendant of the famous Elizabethan freebooter and slaver Sir John Hawkins wore a T-shirt reading "So Sorry" while he knelt in front of a crowd of locals in Gambia.

In Canada, successive federal governments have been apologising and in some cases paying compensation for policies carried out – however distasteful they may be to us now – by their properly constituted predecessors. The practice leads to some interesting questions. Canada used to charge a head tax on immigrants coming from China. Its intent was undoubtedly racist, to discourage "Orientals" from settling in the country. But does present-day Canada have to pay recompense to the descendants of those who chose to pay the head tax? Would it make more sense to use funds for the community as a whole rather than for individuals? How much is enough? Sadly, there have been some unedifying squabbles among different groups claiming to speak for Chinese Canadians about how any government money ought to be distributed.

How far ought we to go in second-guessing, even trying to reverse, the decisions of the past? The British government recently decided that the army should not have executed soldiers for cowardice in World War I. So it has posthumously pardoned them. Is it right, asked Matthew Parris, a respected British journalist, to retrospectively question the judgments made then? "I doubt we are able today to second-guess judgments made three generations ago in different circumstances and according to a harsher moral code," Parris said. Can armies be run without stern discipline, he asks, including harsh reprisals against those who refuse to obey orders or who try to desert in the face of the enemy? It is not natural for human beings to risk death on the battlefield. The threat of execution may help to keep armies from disintegrating into a disorganised rabble. We can say that there should not be wars in the world and that there should not be armies, but until such a peace comes, we need armed forces to defend ourselves and carry out our policies.

Canadian governments have recently indulged in such attempts to refashion the past, over the interning, for example, of particular ethnic groups in wartime. In both world wars, Canada interned those it regarded as enemy nationals. In World War I, it was at war with Austria-Hungary, and many of the Ukrainians living in Canada came from within its borders. Perhaps they had left because they did not like Hapsburg rule; perhaps some of them still felt loyal to the old emperor. In August 1914, indeed, a Ukrainian bishop in Winnipeg urged the men of his flock to head into the United States so that they could make their way home to fight for Franz Josef. Should the Canadian government at the time have taken a chance on their loyalty to their new home? It chose not to and so interned them. The British and Australian governments took a similar view when they interned their German subjects, even though many of them had been resident for decades.

In World War II, Allied governments interned many of those of Japanese, German, and Italian origin. We now know that the Axis powers lost, but at the time the decision was made, it was not at all clear that would happen. And it was not reassuring that all three Axis powers confidently expected help from their emigrant communities in Allied countries. Would it have been responsible of any Allied government to have overlooked the possibility that there might be sympathisers with Nazi Germany, Fascist Italy, or militaristic Japan among them (as indeed there were)? What is less forgivable is that so little attempt was made to distinguish between the loyal and the potentially disloyal. In the United Kingdom a majority of the "enemy aliens" from Germany and Austria were Jewish refugees. Yet they, too, were rounded up and sent to internment camps such as those on the Isle of Man. More than seven thousand were shipped off to Canada and Australia; several hundred died on the *Arandora Star* when it was torpedoed. And what was not responsible and indeed illegal was to seize their property as well. In both the United States and Canada, the property of Japanese internees was stolen, destroyed or sold off at bargain prices to eager speculators. Both governments have since paid compensation.

Words are cheap – although they can lead to expensive demands – and politicians like to appear caring and sensitive. Moreover, apologies about the past can be used as an excuse for not doing very much in the present. Australia has been trying to deal with the grim conditions in which much of its Aboriginal population lives (and Aboriginal life expectancy is seventeen years shorter than that of the rest of the population). Part of that attempt rightly involves looking at the past. In 1997 the country's Human Rights and Equal Opportunity Commission issued a report condemning the long-standing practice, which lasted from World War I into the 1970s, of taking Aboriginal children away from their parents to be brought up as "white." Liberal Australians were horrified, and all the state and territory governments expressed apologies for the "Stolen Generations." In 1998 a citizens' committee held the first annual National Sorry Day, and thousands of Australians signed Sorry Books, which were presented to Aboriginal communities. The Commonwealth government, however, remained silent. John Howard, Australia's prime minister until his defeat in 2007, resisted any suggestion that Australia had anything to apologise for. His successor, Kevin Rudd, brought a motion to the Commonwealth parliament that was unanimously approved. On February 13, 2008, as Aboriginal leaders and other special guests sat in the gallery and Australians all over the country watched on their televisions, Rudd uttered the historic words: "We apologise for the laws and policies of successive Parliaments and governments that have inflicted profound grief, suffering and loss on these our fellow Australians." Yet he carefully avoided the question of compensation and provided few specifics about how the government intends to tackle such problems as illiteracy, drunkenness, child abuse and unemployment among so many Aboriginal communities. One Aboriginal leader was cynical about the possible impact of Rudd's apology: "Blackfellas will get the words, the whitefellas keep the money."

In the United States, a particularly contentious issue has been whether or not the government should apologise for slavery. Blacks and whites divide sharply: while most whites do not feel an apology for what was done generations ago is necessary, an overwhelming majority of blacks think there should be an apology, and a slightly smaller majority think the government should pay compensation to the descendants of slaves. Ninety-six per cent of whites do not think there should be reparations. In his 2000 book, *The Debt: What America Owes to Blacks,* Randall Robinson, a black activist lawyer, argued that much of the prosperity of white America is built on the proceeds of slavery, and he singles out particular institutions such as Brown University whose founders made their fortune by building slave ships. The putative bill is enormous. Richard America, an economist from Georgetown University, has asserted that black Americans are owed somewhere between $5 trillion and $10 trillion. A number of lawsuits seeking compensation for blacks have been filed against American governments and companies, so far without success.

If we look back too much and tinker with history through apologies, the danger is that we do not pay enough attention to the difficult problems of the present. There is also the danger, as a number of minority leaders have pointed out, that focusing on past grievances can be a trap, as governments and groups avoid dealing with issues facing them now. American blacks can demand apologies for slavery and American governments can offer them, but how does that help the black children who are going to poor schools or the black men who cannot find jobs and dignity? Aboriginal Canadians have been preoccupied for decades by their parallel to the "Stolen Generations", the practice of putting native children into boarding schools where they were to learn

English or French and become assimilated into "white" society. According to their many critics, both aboriginal and non-aboriginal, the residential schools, as they are known in Canada, abused the children in their care, sometimes sexually, and stripped them of their culture. Aboriginal leaders have talked of "cultural genocide", and a former United Church clergyman has claimed, so far with little solid proof, to have uncovered evidence of murders, illegal medical experiments, and paedophile rings. The Canadian government has offered compensation to each former student and has set up a Truth and Reconciliation Commission, which will spend five years gathering information and writing its report. Already the chair of the commission is talking of possible criminal charges. Of course, Canadian society must deal with the charges, but it sadly shows little willingness to expend the same resources on dealing with the ghastly conditions on many reserves today. Leon Wieseltier, the distinguished Jewish-American man of letters, warns that the message minority groups too often get from such a focus on the past is: "Don't be fooled ... there is only repression." Dwelling on past horrors such as the Holocaust or slavery can leave people without the resources to deal with problems in the here and now.

3

WHO OWNS THE PAST?

It is particularly unfortunate that just as history is becoming more important in our public discussions, professional historians have largely been abandoning the field to amateurs. The historical profession has turned inward in the last couple of decades, with the result that much historical study today is self-referential. It asks questions about how we, the professional historians, create the past. Which theories do we use or misuse? I remember, while reading applications for graduate school a few years ago, coming across one from what sounded like a bright student who said she wanted to go into a particular field in history because it was "undertheorized".

Perhaps because historians long to sound like their peers in the sciences or the social sciences, they have increasingly gone in for specialised language and long and complex sentences. Much of the writing is difficult, often needlessly so. Andrew Colin Gow, a historian at the University of Alberta, offers a curious defence of obscurantism. We should not, he said severely, expect historians to be entertaining or to tell interesting stories: "Do we need professional history that entertains us – especially when public money pays for so much of what we historians do? Do we need physics that entertains us?"

Historians, however, are not scientists, and if they do not make what they are doing intelligible to the public, then others will rush in to fill the void. Political and other leaders too often get away with misusing or abusing history for their own ends because the rest of us do not know enough to challenge them. Already much of the history that the public reads and enjoys is written by amateur historians. Some of it is very good, but much is not. Bad history tells only part of complex stories. It claims knowledge that it could not possibly have, as when, for example, it purports to give the unspoken thoughts of its characters. Sigmund Freud did his own reputation no good when he teamed up with the American diplomat William Bullitt to write a biography of Woodrow Wilson. Freud never met Wilson, never read his intimate diaries, because Wilson did not keep them, yet he talked confidently of Wilson's obsession with his father and his feelings of failure. Bad history can demand too much of its protagonists, as when it expects them to have had insights or made decisions that they could not possibly have done. Should Europe's statesmen in 1914 have foreseen the stalemate of the western front when virtually all their generals assured them that the war would be over quickly?

Bad history also makes sweeping generalisations for which there is not adequate evidence and ignores awkward facts that do not fit. It used to be thought, for example, that the Treaty of Versailles, made between the Allies and Germany at the end of World War I, was so foolish and vindictive that it led inevitably to World War II. It was a compelling story, bolstered by the polemics of men such as John Maynard Keynes, but it overlooked a few considerations. Germany *had* lost the war, and its treatment was never as severe as many Germans claimed and many British and Americans came to believe. Reparations were a burden but never as great as they seemed. Germany paid a fraction of the bill, and when Hitler came to power, he cancelled it outright. If Germany in the 1920s had financial problems, it was largely due to the fiscal policies of the German government, which wanted to neither raise taxes nor default on the war bonds that so many of its own middle class held. What is more, things were getting better in the 1920s, not worse. Europe and the world were recovering economically, and Germany and even Soviet Russia were being brought into the international system. Without the Great Depression, which put fearful strains on even the strongest democracies, and without a whole series of bad decisions, including those by respectable German statesmen and generals who thought they could use Hitler once they got him into power, the slide into aggression and then war might not have occurred. Bad history ignores such nuances in favor of tales that belong to morality plays but do not help us to consider the past in all its complexity. The lessons such history teaches are too simple or simply wrong. That is why we need to learn how to evaluate it properly and to treat the claims made in its name with scepticism.

Professional historians ought not to surrender their territory so easily. We must do our best to raise the public awareness of the past in all its richness and complexity. We must contest the one-sided, even false, histories that are out there in the public domain. If we do not, we allow our leaders and opinion-makers to use history to bolster false claims and justify bad and foolish policies. Furthermore, historians must not abandon political history entirely for sociology or cultural studies. Like it or not, politics matters to our societies and to our lives. We need only ask ourselves how different the world would have been if Hitler and the Nazis had not seized control of one of Europe's most powerful states. Or what could have happened to American capitalism and the American people if Franklin Delano Roosevelt had not been able, as president, to implement the New Deal.

While it is instructive, informative, and indeed fun to study such subjects as the carnivals in the French Revolution, the image of the Virgin Mary in the Middle Ages, the role of the doughnut in the Canadian psyche (Canadians apparently eat more per capita than anyone else in the world), or the hamburger in American life, we ought not to forget the aspect of history that the great nineteenth-century German historian Leopold von Ranke summed up as "what really happened".

Every generation has its own preoccupations and concerns and therefore looks for new things in the past and asks different questions. When I was an undergraduate, our standard texts dealt with political and economic history. There was little social history and certainly no gender history. The first wave of feminism in the late 1960s produced an interest in women's history. The growth of the gay rights movement brought a corresponding growth in gay and lesbian history. The preoccupations of the baby boom generation with, for example, remaining young and attractive have given rise to such specialised subjects as the history of the body. The disappearance of the European empires and the rise of Asia in economic and political power have produced global history less centred on Europe and North America. That process of researching and writing about the new questions we ask of the past is what makes history change and develop.

Nevertheless, there is an irreducible core to the story of the past, and that is, what happened and in what order? Causality and sequence are crucial to understanding the past. We cannot argue that Napoleon actually won the Battle of Waterloo or that the battle took place before his invasions of Russia or Spain, although we can certainly disagree about why he lost at Waterloo and how much those earlier decisions of his contributed to his defeat. If we do not, as historians, write the history of great events as well as the small stories that make up the past, others will, and they will not necessarily do it well.

Historians, especially in the past, have done their share of creating bad and tendentious histories. In the Middle Ages, Christian historians saw the past in terms of the triumph of the universal Catholic Church. When a Renaissance scholar showed that the document which purported to hand on the power of the Roman emperors to the pope was a fake, his work helped to stimulate a fresh look at that assumption. Victorian historians too often depicted the past as an inevitable progress leading to the glorious present when Britain ruled the world. And French and German and Russian and American historians did much the same thing for their nations' stories. Like epic poems, their books were filled with heroes and villains and stirring events. Such histories, says Michael Howard, the eminent British historian, sustain us in difficult times, but they are "nursery history."

The proper role for historians, Howard rightly says, is to challenge and even explode national myths: "Such disillusion is a necessary part of growing up in and belonging to an adult society; and a good definition of the difference between a Western liberal society and a totalitarian one – whether it is Communist, Fascist, or Catholic authoritarian – is that in the former the government treats its citizens as responsible adults and in the latter it cannot." After World War II, most Western democracies made the difficult but wise decision to commission proper military histories of the conflict. In other words, they hired professional historians and gave them unrestricted access to the archives. The results were histories which did not gloss over Allied mistakes and failures but which strove to give as full a picture as possible of a great and complicated struggle.

The British case is an interesting one. The government

initially gave Winston Churchill free run of the records (and a very advantageous tax deal) to allow him to write his great history of World War II. Part of its aim was to make sure that a British account of the war got into print before the inevitable rush of memoirs and histories from the United States and Russia. The result, as David Reynolds has so convincingly shown, was a sweeping and magisterial account which glossed over many awkward issues. Churchill said little, for example, of the debates within the British cabinet in those dark days of May 1940. France had fallen to the Nazis, and, according to Churchill's account, there was no discussion of what Britain should do, only unanimity that it must fight on alone. "Future generations", he wrote, "may deem it noteworthy that the supreme question of whether we should fight on alone never found a place upon the War Cabinet agenda. It was taken for granted and as a matter of course by these men of all parties in the State, and we were much too busy to waste time upon such unreal, academic issues." In fact, as the record shows, the cabinet properly considered alternatives, most notably to see if Benito Mussolini, the Italian dictator, could broker a peace. When that was rightly rejected as unlikely to lead to anything useful and, moreover, ran the risk of dealing a serious blow to British morale, the cabinet made its momentous decision.

From the start of the war, however, the British government had also intended that there would be an official history, and in 1946 it appointed Sir James Butler, a respected historian, to oversee what was expected to be a series of volumes on different aspects of the British war effort. Butler made it clear that for the sake of the reputation of the series, he wanted to be able to select individual contributors who were reputable and independent academics, not military specialists. Furthermore, his historians were to have complete access to the written record and a free hand to use what they found, provided it did not jeopardise national security. As a consequence, the British official histories are informative, frank, and at times controversial. The one on the bomber offensive against Germany, for example, deals bluntly with the disagreements in the air force's high command over whether area bombing, which was preferred, or precision bombing was the most effective way of damaging Germany. What that former strategy meant in practice was to target cities and towns rather than smaller sites, such as munitions factories or oil depots. When the Air Ministry objected in 1959 to the volume on the grounds that revealing such debates might damage the Royal Air Force, the secretary to the cabinet, Sir Norman Brook, gave a firm answer. The histories, he argued, were not meant to whitewash the record. Rather, by dealing with the difficult issues, they would help future governments learn from past mistakes.

Blunt histories do not always meet with warm approval. Noble Frankland, the historian who wrote the official history of the bombing campaign, found himself the subject of vicious personal attacks. Although he had himself flown in the campaign and won the Distinguished Flying Cross, the conservative press in the United Kingdom insinuated that he had been judged unfit. (He had in fact been grounded for about eight weeks with pneumonia, after which he went back into the air over Germany.) Frankland, his critics wrongly claimed, had not been there, and only those who had taken part in the fighting could possibly understand it. Many of his most vociferous critics admitted that they had not read his book or had read only parts of it, but that did not inhibit them in the slightest. Frankland's suggestions that the resources used in the bombing might have been better applied elsewhere in the last months of the war, or that its effectiveness in destroying German morale was open to question, were rapidly inflated into charges that he had called the whole campaign "a costly failure", words he certainly never used. He was insulting, it was claimed, the memory of all those who had died and hurting the feelings of the survivors and their families. He was, said one member of Parliament, typical of those cynical and unscrupulous writers who hoped to make money by writing sensational exposés. The charges levelled against Frankland find a parallel in those being made today about the Canadian War Museum's exhibit on the same bombing campaign. The museum, its critics say, has wrongly suggested in a plaque titled "An Enduring Controversy" that the mass bombing of German industry and German cities and towns was both immoral and ineffective. What the plaque actually said was, "The value and morality of the strategic bomber offensive against Germany remains bitterly contested".

As so often is the case, the ways the public reacts to the work of historians have much to do with the issues of the time. In the late 1950s, Britain was going through a painful period of re-examination as it adjusted to its diminished importance in the world and its manifest social and economic problems at home. The Suez adventure of 1956 had been a costly disaster, and although the new Conservative prime minister, Harold Macmillan, made much of his nation's special relationship with the United States, it was quite clear which country was the dominant partner. The empire was melting away; indeed, Macmillan had just made his famous speech about the wind of change blowing through Africa when he had to decide whether or not to let Frankland's volume be published. World War II assumed ever greater importance as the glorious and gallant moment when all British pulled together and Britain was one of the Big Three powers. The mix of nostalgia and pride was neatly and unkindly caught by the satirical revue *Beyond the Fringe* in its sketch "Aftermyth of War". Frankland's careful and clear examination of the bombing campaign and his revelations about the debates and disputes that had gone on at the time came as a dash of cold water.

Historians, the great philosopher of history R. G. Colling-wood wrote in his autobiography, examine the past with a careful eye, even if it means exploding cherished myths: "So long as the past and the present are outside one another, knowledge of the past is not of much use in the present. But suppose the past lives on in the present; suppose, though encapsulated in it, and at first sight hidden beneath the present's contradictory and more prominent features, it is still alive and active; the historian may very well be related to the non-historian as the trained woodsman is to the ignorant traveller." That can often be intensely irritating when the historians raise qualifications and point to ambiguities. Do we really want to know that our great heroes, such as Winston Churchill, made silly mistakes? That there was and is a controversy over the effectiveness and morality of the World War II Allied bombing campaign against Germany? That John F. Kennedy suffered from a variety of illnesses and was dangerously dependent on painkillers? I think we do, not for prurient reasons, but because a complex picture is more satisfying for adults than a simplistic one. We can still have heroes, still have views on the rights and wrongs of the past, and still be glad that it turned out in one way rather than another; but we have to accept that in history, as in our own lives, very little is absolutely black or absolutely white.

Historians, of course, do not own the past. We all do. But because historians spend their time studying history, they are in a better position than most amateurs to make reasoned judgments. Historians, after all, are trained to ask questions, make connections, and collect and examine the evidence. Ideally, they already possess a considerable body of knowledge and an understanding of the context of particular times or events. Yet when they produce work that challenges deeply held beliefs and myths about the past, they are often accused of being elitist, nihilistic, or simply out of touch with that imaginary place, "the real world". In the case of recent history, they are also told, as Noble Frankland was, that they cannot have an opinion if they were not there.

The idea that those who actually took part in great events or lived through particular times have a superior understanding to those who come later is a deeply held yet wrong-headed one. The recent dispute at Canada's War Museum over the Allied bombing campaign has predictably brought charges that the historians who mounted the exhibit and those who supported it must defer to the views of the veteran airmen. Of course, said the *National Post,* "there is the issue of free expression and not caving into the sensitivities of every special interest group. Veterans, though, are not just any special interest group". I was one of the outside historians called in to evaluate the exhibit when the fuss started. (I supported the plaque and strongly advised the War Museum not to back down.) When my views became known, I started to get mail saying that I had no authority to comment on World War II because I was not part of it. And, as a woman, it was hinted, what could I know of things military anyway? True, I did not receive the e-mail that one of my colleagues did: "The veterans have done more for our country and way of life, and shown more courage and dedication to duty, than you ever will. Since they were there, and you were not, it stands to reason that they should have the final say as to whether or not the plaque is fair."

Being there does not necessarily give greater insight into events; indeed, sometimes the opposite is true. I lived through the Cuban missile crisis, for example, but at the time I knew only what was reported in the media. Like millions of others, I knew nothing of the intense debates in Washington and Moscow about how to handle the crisis. I had no idea that Kennedy had secret channels of communication with the Soviets or that the Soviets already had nuclear warheads in Cuba. I did not know that Fidel

Castro was prepared to see his country destroyed if it brought Soviet victory in the Cold War closer. It was only much later, as the classified documents started to appear on both sides, that we got a much more detailed and comprehensive view of what was really happening. The same gap exists between the experiences of the veterans and the history of the bombing campaign. They knew what it was like to risk their lives flying over Germany, but they could not know about the debates in Whitehall or the impact of the bombs they dropped. That could only come with hindsight and much research and analysis.

Memory, as psychologists tell us, is a tricky business. It is true that we all remember bits of the past, often in vivid detail. We can recall what we wore and said on particular occasions, or sights, smells, tastes and sounds. But we do not always remember accurately. Dean Acheson, the distinguished American statesman, once told the historian Arthur Schlesinger Jr. that he needed a strong martini after spending a morning on his memoirs. Acheson had been sketching out the run-up to Pearl Harbor and remembered vividly being in President Roosevelt's office with the president and Cordell Hull, then secretary of state, on that fateful day in 1941 when the United States took a step closer to war with Japan by freezing Japanese assets. "The President was sitting at his desk; Cordell Hull was sitting opposite him; I was in a chair at the Secretary's side", he had written. The only trouble was that his secretary had checked the records and found that Hull had not even been in Washington that day.

We mistakenly think that memories are like carvings in stone; once done, they do not change. Nothing could be further from the truth. Memory is not only selective; it is malleable. In the 1990s, there was much public concern and excitement about recovered memories. Authoritative figures published books and appeared in the media claiming that it was possible to completely repress memories of painful and traumatic events. Working with therapists, a number of patients discovered memories of such ghastly things as sexual abuse by their parents, cannibalism, satanic cults and murder. Many families were destroyed and lives, both of the accusers and of the accused, ruined. Now that the panic has died down, we are ruefully admitting that there is no evidence at all that human beings repress painful memories. If anything, the memories remain particularly vivid.

Researchers at the Biological Psychiatry Lab at McLean Hospital, affiliated with the Harvard Medical School, have recently conducted a research project into the repressed-memory syndrome. Their interest was piqued by its sudden appearance in the late twentieth century. If the syndrome were hardwired into the human brain, then surely there would be evidence of its occurrence down through history. They found examples in nineteenth-century literature, but, although they offered rewards, they turned up no examples either in fiction or in non-fiction before 1800. They concluded that "the phenomenon is not a natural neurological function, but rather a 'culture-bound' syndrome rooted in the nineteenth century". The preoccupation of the Romantics with the supernatural and the imagination, as well as later work, most notably that of Sigmund Freud, into the subconscious, predisposed us to believe that the mind can play extraordinary tricks on us.

We edit our memories over the years partly out of a natural human instinct to make our own roles more attractive or important. But we also change them because times and attitudes change over the years. In the early years after World War I, the dead were commemorated in France and Britain as fallen heroes who had fought to defend their civilisation. It was only later as disillusionment about the war grew that the British and French publics came to remember them as the victims of a futile struggle. We also edit out of our memories what no longer seems appropriate or right. When I interviewed British women who had lived in India as part of the Raj, I always asked them what the relations between the British rulers and their Indian subjects were like. They all invariably told me that there was never any tension between the races and that the British never expressed racist views. Yet we know from contemporary sources – letters, for example, or diaries – that many, perhaps most, of the British in India saw Indians as their inferiors.

We also polish our memories in the recounting. Primo Levi, who did so much to keep the memory of the Nazi concentration camps alive, warned, "A memory evoked too often, and expressed in the form of a story, tends to become fixed in stereotype . . . crystallised, perfected, adorned, installing itself in the place of the raw memory and growing at its expense". As we learn more about the past, that knowledge can become part of our memory, too. The director of the Yad Vashem memorial to the Holocaust in Israel once said sadly that most of the oral histories that had been collected were unreliable. Holocaust survivors thought, for example, that they remembered witnessing well-known atrocities when in fact they were nowhere near the place where the events happened.

In the 1920s, the French sociologist Maurice Halbwachs coined the term "collective memory" for the things we think we know for certain about the past of our own societies. "Typically", he wrote, "a collective memory, at least a significant collective memory, is understood to express some eternal or essential truth about the group – usually tragic". So the Poles remember the partitions of their country – "the Christ among nations" – in the eighteenth century as part of their martyrdom as a nation. The Serbs remember the Battle of Kosovo in 1389 as their defeat on earth but their moral victory in their unending struggle against Muslims. Often present-day concerns affect what we remember as a group. Kosovo acquired its particularly deep significance in the memory of the Serbs as they were struggling to become an independent nation in the nineteenth century. In earlier centuries, the battle was remembered as one incident in a much larger story. Collective memory is more about the present than the past because it is integral to how a group sees itself. And what that memory is can be and often is the subject of debate and argument where, in Halbwachs's words, "competing narratives about central symbols in the collective past, and the collectivity's relationship to that past, are disputed and negotiated in the interest of redefining the collective present".

Peter Novick has argued forcefully in his book *The Holocaust in American Life* that for American Jews, the Holocaust became a central identifying feature of who they were only in the 1960s. In the years after World War II, few American Jews wanted to remember that their co-religionists had been victims. Jewish organisations urged their community to look to the future and not the past. It was only in the 1960s that attitudes began to change, partly, Novick argues, because victimhood began to acquire a more positive status and partly because the 1967 and 1973 wars showed both Israel's strength and its continuing vulnerability.

As the nineteenth-century Zionists began their bold project of re-creating a Jewish state, they looked to Jewish history for symbols and lessons. They found, among much else, the story of Masada. In A.D. 73, as the Romans stamped out the last remnants of Jewish resistance to their rule, a band of some thousand men, women and children held out on the hilltop fortress of Masada. When it became clear that the garrison was doomed, its leader, Elazar Ben-Yair, convinced the men that it was better to die than submit to Rome. The men killed their women and children and then themselves. The story was recorded but did not assume importance for Jews until the modern age. Masada has been taken up as a symbol not of submission to an inevitable fate but of the determination of the Jewish people to die if necessary in their struggle for freedom. In independent Israel, it became an inspiration and a site of pilgrimage for the Israeli military as well as for civilians. As a popular poem has it, "Never again shall Masada fall!" In recent years, as pessimism has grown in Israel over the prospects for peace with its neighbours, another collective memory about Masada has been taking shape: that it is a warning that Jews always face persecution at the hands of their enemies.

While collective memory is usually grounded in fact, it need not be. If you go to China, you will more than likely be told the story of the park in the foreign concession area of Shanghai which had on its gate a sign that read, "Dogs and Chinese Not Admitted." While it is true that the park was reserved for foreigners, insulting enough in itself, the real insult for most Chinese was their pairing with dogs. The only trouble is that there is no evidence the sign ever existed. When young Chinese historians expressed some doubts about the story in 1994, the official press reacted with anger. "Some people", a well-known journalist wrote, "do not understand the humiliations of old China's history or else they harbour sceptical attitudes and even go so far as to write off serious historical humiliation lightly; this is very dangerous".

It can be dangerous to question the stories people tell about themselves because so much of our identity is both shaped by and bound up with our history. That is why dealing with the past, in deciding on which version we want, or on what we want to remember and to forget, can become so politically charged.

4

HISTORY AND

IDENTITY

We argue over history in part because it can have real significance in the present. We use it in a variety of ways: to mobilise ourselves to achieve goals in the future, to make claims – for land, for example – and, sadly, to attack and belittle others. Examining the past can be a sort of therapy as we uncover knowledge about our own societies that has been overlooked or repressed. For those who do not have power or who feel that they do not have enough, history can be a way of protesting against their marginalisation, or against trends or ideas they do not like, such as globalisation. Histories that show past injustices or crimes can be used to argue for redress in the present. For all of us, the powerful and weak alike, history helps to define and validate us.

Who am I? is one question we ask ourselves, but equally important is, who are we? We obtain much of our identity from the communities into which we are born or to which we choose to belong. Gender, ethnicity, sexual orientation, age, class, nationality, religion, family, clan, geography, occupation and, of course, history can go into the ways that we define our identity. As new ways of defining ourselves appear, so do new communities. The idea of the teenager, for example, scarcely existed before 1900. People were either adults or children. In the twentieth century, in developed countries, children were staying in school much longer and hence were more dependent on their parents. The adolescent years became a long bridge between childhood and full adulthood. The market spotted an opportunity, and so we got special teenage clothes, music, magazines, books and television and radio shows.

We see ourselves as individuals but equally as parts of groups. Sometimes our group is small, an extended family perhaps, sometimes vast. Benedict Anderson has coined the memorable phrase "imagined communities" for the groups, like nations or religions, that are so big that we can never know all the other members yet which still draw our loyalties. Groups mark out their identities by symbols, whether flags, coloured shirts, or special songs. In that process of definition, history usually plays a key role. Army regiments have long understood the importance of history in creating a sense of cohesiveness. That is why they have regimental histories and battle honors from past campaigns. Not surprisingly, the stories from the past that are celebrated are often one-sided or simplistic.

Most Americans know the story of Paul Revere's ride: the brave patriot galloping alone through that night in 1775 to warn his fellow revolutionaries that the British redcoats were about to attack. Eight decades later Henry Wadsworth Longfellow helped to fix the ride in American memories with his epic poem. To the regret of historians, he got some of the key details wrong. Revere did not, for example, put the lanterns to signal the movements of the British ("one if by land, and two if by sea") in the steeple of the Old North Church. Rather, they were a signal to him. Most important, perhaps, he acted not on his own but as part of a well-planned, well-coordinated strategy. Several riders went out that night, in different directions. David Hackett Fischer, who has written what is the definitive study on the ride, finds this truer version preferable to the Longfellow one. "The more we learn about these messengers, the more interesting Paul Revere's part becomes – not merely as a solitary courier, but as an organiser and promoter of a common effort in the cause of freedom."

Historians have also been examining the myth of the American West. Hundreds of Western movies and thousands of novels by writers such as Zane Grey (who only went west on his honeymoon) and Karl May (who never went there at all) have helped to create a picture of a wild world where bold cowboys and determined settlers braved savage Indian hordes. The myth casts a powerful spell. From President Teddy Roosevelt to President George W. Bush, American political elites have liked to portray themselves as bold cowboys. Even Henry Kissinger, improbable as the image may seem, once fell under the spell. "Americans like the cowboy who leads the wagon train by riding ahead alone on his horse", he told the Italian journalist Oriana Fallaci. "He acts, that's all, by being in the right place at the right time." Yet the "real" old West, the time of the wagon trains moving through the ever-open and lawless frontier, lasted for a surprisingly short time, roughly from the 1840s, when settlers in increasing numbers moved west of the Missouri River, to the opening of the first transcontinental railway in 1869. Moreover, many of the familiar stereotypes dissolve into something more complex and even disturbing. The cowboys were often teenage gunslingers who today might well be in urban gangs or in jail. Billy the Kid was a charming and cold-blooded killer. Miss Kitty Russell, the warm and attractive saloon owner in the television series *Gunsmoke*, would have looked quite different in the real old West. Women of her sort on the frontier were miserable low-paid prostitutes, frequently drunk and riddled with diseases. Many of them killed themselves.

Within the United States, the national organising myths have been challenged by strong regional ones, particularly in the case of the South. Whites in the American South developed their own distinctive history after the Civil War. Not surprisingly, the old prewar South took on a golden glow, where men were gentlemen and women ladies, where gentility and courtesy marked relations among people, even between slave owners and their slaves. The Yankee victory brought an end to a civilisation, and Reconstruction caused only loss and degradation. The United Daughters of the Confederacy, set up in 1894, were vigilant in monitoring school curricula to ensure that their approved version of the past was taught in Southern schools. Textbook publishers complied, publishing different versions of the American history texts: one for the South, which downplayed slavery and ignored its brutality, and the other for Northern schools. And so, even black children in their segregated schools were presented with a picture of the South in which slavery and racism were largely absent. They were told, though, that Africans were fortunate because they had been brought to America and so into contact with European civilisation. It was a pity, the texts concluded sadly, that the Africans had not had the innate capacity to take advantage of the opportunity. Black teachers did their best to counteract such views by introducing African and African American history into their schools, but it was not always easy because the curricula had to be approved by white school boards.

Public commemorations, museums, and archives reinforced the white version of Southern history. Throughout the South, such public spaces as parks and squares were named after Confederate heroes and filled with their monuments. In 1957, the state of Virginia held a ceremony to celebrate the 350th anniver-

sary of the first settlement at Jamestown. The past being celebrated was entirely white; there was no mention of the local Indians or the African slaves who were going to be brought there a
few years afterward. No blacks were among the invited guests in
1957; six had been invited by mistake, but their invitations had
been hastily rescinded.

In the 1960s, with the growth of the civil rights movement, the
balance of power in the South began to shift and Southern history
shifted along with it. As state after state integrated its schools, the
old-style textbooks became an embarrassment. Museums started
to acknowledge the black presence in the South in their displays
and exhibitions. It was surely a sign of changing times when the
Museum of the Confederacy put leg irons on display. Southern
blacks pushed to get their own museums of black history and the
history of civil rights. Their task was not always easy, and not just
because of diehard white opposition. Because black history had not
been valued by white-dominated institutions, much documentation
and many artefacts which could have illuminated the history of
blacks in the South had simply not survived. Blacks increasingly
demanded that their heroes be commemorated in public spaces.
In Richmond, Virginia, which first elected a black-majority city
council in 1977, a monument to the great black tennis player
Arthur Ashe has been added to those to Civil War heroes along
Monument Avenue, and in 2000 two bridges over the Potomac
named after the great Civil War soldiers Stonewall Jackson and
Jeb Stuart were renamed after local civil rights fighters.

Recently whites and blacks in the South have tried to share a
common history. In 1999 blacks and whites stood together at the
unveiling of a roadside plaque to mark the lynching of two
black couples half a century before. It was the first time the in-
famous history of lynching had been publicly recognised in
Georgia. "It is time", said a local paper, "to heal the wounds". In

Williamsburg, Virginia, where the carefully preserved colonial town once had no reference to its large slave population and where the historical re-enactments showed only whites, the newer history depicts the relationship between slaves and slave owners. At times angry tourists have intervened when beatings of runaway slaves, for example, have been too realistic. And not everyone appreciates the more rounded view of the past. History, many maintain, should be uplifting, not depressing. Opponents of a monument in Virginia to a failed slave revolt argued that it was glorifying violence.

Feeling part of something, in our fluid and uncertain times, can be comforting. If we are Christians, Muslims, Canadians, Scots, or gays, it implies that we belong to something larger, more stable, and more enduring than ourselves. Our group predated us and will presumably survive our deaths. When many of us no longer believe in an afterlife, that promises us a sort of immortality. Identity, though, can also be a trap which imprisons us and divides us from others. Victorian boys used to be told, "Don't cry, you are a little Englishman." Women repeatedly have been told that as members of a particular community, they must be meek and submissive. Neighbours are told not to trust one another because they are Serbs or Croats, Muslims or Jews. In Toronto, where I grew up, Protestants and Catholics went to separate schools. It used to be a matter of scandal and shame if a member of one community chose to marry a member of the other.

History is a way of enforcing the imagined community. Nationalists, to take one example, like to claim that their nation has always existed back into that conveniently vague area, "the mists of time." The Anglican Church claims that in spite of the break with Rome during the Reformation, it is part of an unbroken progression from the early Church. In reality, an examination of any group shows that its identity is a process, not a fixed thing. Groups define and redefine themselves over time and in response to internal developments, a religious awakening, perhaps, or outside pressures. If you are oppressed and victimised, as gays have been and still are in many societies, that becomes part of how you see yourself. Sometimes that leads to an unseemly competition for victimhood. American blacks have watched resentfully as the commemoration of the Holocaust has taken an ever greater place in American consciousness. Was not slavery just as great a crime? some have asked.

When previously marginal or ignored groups develop a sense of themselves, the past inevitably comes into play. When women and gays started to push for greater rights, for example, their histories also developed. Examining the ways in which women and gays were disadvantaged in the past or how they coped, or by discovering and telling the stories of earlier feminists or gay activists, historians helped to create a sense of solidarity and even a sense of entitlement to some form of compensation.

In the 1920s, the black American educator and historian Carter G. Woodson started the Negro History Week to challenge white stereotypes about blacks, in part by highlighting black achievements. By the 1970s, American blacks had successfully asserted their rights through the civil rights movement and were increasingly taking pride in being black. In 1976, as the United States celebrated its bicentennial, Woodson's week became Black History Month. President Gerald Ford sent a message of goodwill: "The last quarter-century has finally witnessed significant strides in the full integration of black people into every area of national life. In celebrating Black History Month, we can take satisfaction from this recent progress in the realisation of the ideals envisioned by our Founding Fathers. But, even more than this, we can seize the opportunity to honour the too-often-neglected accomplishments of black Americans in every area of endeavour throughout our history." The aims of the equivalent month in the United Kingdom similarly are to celebrate black contributions to British society and encourage blacks to feel pride in their own culture. In Canada, in the 1990s, black parents argued that local schools did not say enough about the contribution of blacks in Canada. "Africans in America were held on the outside", said the director of the Black Cultural Centre in Nova Scotia. Now, with blacks entering the mainstream, they needed to know their history. For other black leaders, their history was a way of coping with a hostile world and overcoming stereotypes. In 1995, in response to pressure from Canadian blacks, the government decreed that Canada have its own Black History Month, "to celebrate the many achievements and contributions of Black Canadians, who, throughout history, have done so much to make Canada the culturally diverse, compassionate and prosperous nation we know today".

Today deaf activists, who argue that being deaf is not a disability but a distinguishing mark of separateness, are in the process of creating a Deaf Nation. They resist medical interventions, such as cochlear implants, or attempts to train deaf children to speak ("Oralism", they say with contempt) and insist that sign language is a fully fledged language in its own right. Capitalising the *D* in "Deaf" symbolises the view that deafness is a culture and not simply the loss of hearing. Scholars give papers and teach courses on Deaf history and publish books with titles such as *Deaf Heritage in Canada: A Distinctive, Diverse, and Enduring Culture* or *Britain's Deaf Heritage*. In 1984, an American professor named Harlan Lane started researching and publishing about the oppression of the deaf in the past. Although he himself can hear, he is learning sign language.

Today, those who count themselves Deaf often wear a blue ribbon because that is what the Nazis made the deaf wear. At a formal blue ribbon ceremony in Australia in 1999, seven Deaf narrators carrying candles spoke of their culture, their history, and their survival as a community. "We remember those Deaf people who were victims of Oralism in their education, denied their sign languages and Deaf teachers." And, he went on, "we remember the constant attempts either to eliminate us or to prevent us from being born, by not allowing Deaf people to marry each other, through enforced sterilisation". At a recent Deaf convention in the United Kingdom, Lane told his British audience that speech therapists and hearing-aid manufacturers in the United States have coalesced into a powerful lobby to grind the deaf minority down. Paddy Ladd, an equally impassioned British professor who is himself deaf, praises the nineteenth-century deaf French scholar Ferdinand Berthier, whose attempts to build an international deaf community, Ladd says, were thwarted by oral imperialists. There was an earlier, happier time, even a golden age, so Deaf history has it, when a venerable French priest set up a school for deaf children in the second half of the eighteenth century and understood that they must have their own sign language. Unfortunately, for the Deaf activists, the record shows that he intended signing to be not an end in itself but a stage on the way to teaching his pupils to lip-read and perhaps even speak.

Lost golden ages can be very effective tools for motivating people in the present. "Unity was and is the destiny of Italy", Giuseppe Mazzini, the great nineteenth-century Italian nationalist, urged the divided peninsula. "The civil primacy, twice exercised by Italy – through the arms of the Caesars and the voice of the Popes – is destined to be held a third time by the people of Italy – the nation." Mazzini was also a liberal who believed that a world filled by self-governing peoples would be a happy, democratic, and peaceful one, yet there was an ominous tone to his exhortations: "They who were unable forty years ago to perceive the signs of progress towards unity made in the successive periods of Italian life, were simply blind to the light of History. But should any, in the face of the actual glorious manifestation of our people, endeavour to lead them back to ideas of confederations, and independent provincial liberty, they would deserve to be branded as traitors to their country." A great past can be a promise, but it can also be a terrible burden. Mussolini promised the Italians a second Roman Empire and led them to disaster in World War II.

Greek nationalists in the early nineteenth century, and their supporters in Europe, took it for granted that they were freeing the heirs of classical Greek civilisation from the Ottoman Empire. Surely history would grant them a second chance. Greek scholars wrote books showing that there was a direct line from the classical world to the modern. (The four centuries of Ottoman rule were largely overlooked.) Foreign scholars who suggested that such a view was too simplistic were pilloried or ignored. Written Greek was modelled on the classical, and so generations of schoolchildren struggled with a language which was very different from the one they spoke. It was only in 1976 that the government finally conceded and made modern Greek the official language. More dangerously, the past held the promise of a reborn Greek empire. Eleuthérios Venizélos, the leading Greek statesman at the time of World War I, once gathered his friends around a map and drew the outlines of ancient Greece, at the height of its influence, across the modern borders. His outline included most of modern Turkey, a good part of Albania, and most of the islands of the eastern Mediterranean. (He could also have included parts of Italy, but did not.) Under the influence of that great (*megali*) idea, he sent Greek soldiers to Asia Minor in 1919 to stake out Greece's claims. The result was a catastrophe for the

Greek armies and for all those innocent Greeks who had lived for generations in what became modern Turkey. As the resurgent Turkish armies under Kemal Atatürk pressed the Greek forces back, hundreds of thousands of bewildered refugees, many of whom barely knew Greek, followed them. In turn, huge numbers of Turks, many distinguished from their Greek neighbours only by their religion, abandoned their homes and villages for Turkey. The events of those years have in turn become part of history and have poisoned relations between Greece and Turkey up to the present.

Ideologies call on history as well, but in their hands the past becomes a prophecy. The faithful may have suffered, and may be suffering still, but history is moving toward a preordained end. Whether secular like Marxism or Fascism, or religious like the fundamentalisms of various faiths, the story they tell is at once breathtakingly simple and all-encompassing. Every event is fitted into the grand account and all is explained. The writer Arthur Koestler remembered the great relief and delight he felt when he discovered Marxism in the troubled years when the Weimar Republic was failing and the Nazis were reaching out for power. Past, present, and future all became comprehensible: "The new light seems to pour from all directions across the skull; the whole universe falls into pattern like the stray pieces of a jigsaw puzzle assembled at one stroke."

Karl Marx believed that he had discovered that history had laws just as science does and that these showed a Communist future was bound to come. History had started with primitive communism, an idyllic world of hunters and gatherers where there was no private property but everyone shared everything according to need. The end of history, Marx promised, was a similar society but this time, thanks to new and improved types of production, a much more prosperous one. Fascism, like

Communism, saw itself as facing the future, but it, too, called on old emotions and memories. The Nazis made much of ancient myths and legends and of historical figures such as Frederick the Great; Frederick Barbarossa, who was crowned German king in the twelfth century; and the contemporaneous Teutonic Knights, whose crusades included not only the Holy Land but also much of the Baltic. These were all supposed to show the genius and continuity of the German race – and the need for it to resume its onward march. "We take up where we left off six hundred years ago", wrote Hitler in *Mein Kampf*. "We stop the endless German movements to the south and the west, and turn our gaze towards the land in the east." Religious fundamentalists, of course, do much the same as they summon believers back to the "true" religion as it first was after the divine revelations. They, too, paint a golden age when all the faithful lived in harmony, obeying the laws they had been given. Muslim fundamentalists, for example, want to revive the caliphate and bring in sharia law (although deciding which of the several schools of sharia may be difficult).

Setbacks and defeats become parts of such stories, rather than challenges to their truth. If the faithful have suffered, that is because of the plots and conspiracies of their enemies. For Hitler, of course, that meant the Jews. They had started World War I and created the Bolshevik Revolution, and they had ensured that Germany suffered under the Treaty of Versailles. He had warned them, Hitler said repeatedly, that if they dared to start another war, he would destroy them, "the vermin of Europe". World War II was the fault of the Jews, and the time had come to deal with them once and for all. If any one person was responsible for that war, it was Hitler himself, but logic and reason do not enter into closed systems of viewing the world. In 1991, the American tele-vangelist Pat Robertson warned that Bush Sr.'s victory over Iraq was not what it appeared. It was paving the way not for peace but for the triumph of evil. It was all so clear to Robertson. Ever since the Bolshevik Revolution of 1917, a secret conspiracy had been pushing the world toward socialism and the triumph of the Antichrist. The European Union was clearly part of the plot and so was the United Nations. The Gulf War and the missiles that Saddam Hussein had fired on Israel were yet more steps toward the final reckoning.

Remembering the evils of the past helps to sustain the faithful. Yes, the present may look dark, but that, too, is part of the story before the triumph of the faithful and paradise comes on earth or in heaven. A few weeks after September 11, 2001, Osama bin Laden released a tape in which he exulted about the destruction of the World Trade Center towers: "Our Islamic nation has been tasting the same for more than eighty years, of humiliation and disgrace, its sons killed and their blood spilled, its sanctities desecrated." Few people in the West knew that for him, Muslim degradation had started in the modern age with the abolition of the caliphate. In 1924, in a move which caused little comment in the West, Atatürk, the founder of a new and secular Turkey, had abolished that last office held by the deposed Ottoman sultans. As caliphs, they had claimed spiritual leadership of the world's Muslims. The last one, a gentle poet, had gone quietly into exile. For many Muslims, from India to the Middle East, the abolition was a blow to their dream of a united Muslim world governed according to God's laws. For bin Laden and those who thought like him, disunity among Muslims had allowed Western powers to push the Middle East around; to take its oil and, with the establishment of Israel, its land; to corrupt its leaders; and to lead ordinary Muslims astray. The Saudi rulers had committed the ultimate sin of allowing the United States to bring its troops onto the holy land where Muslims had their most sacred sites. Bin Laden's history includes much more than the past eighty years.

The Crusades, the defeat of the Moors in Spain, Western imperialism in the nineteenth century, and the evils of the twentieth all add up to a dark tale of Muslim humiliation and suffering. Such history keeps followers angry and motivated and attracts new recruits.

While most of us do not take such a simple view of the world, we nevertheless find history can be useful to justify what we are doing in the present. In 2007, Canada's prime minister, Stephen Harper, paid a visit to France for the rededication of the Vimy Ridge war memorial to the many Canadian soldiers who had died there in 1917. Canadians were uneasy with his government's support for the Bush war on terror and with the mounting losses being suffered by Canadian troops in Afghanistan. Harper had already made it clear where he stood: Canada's interest lay in backing Washington on virtually every major international issue, and he intended to keep Canadian forces in Afghanistan for the foreseeable future. In his speech he underlined how the capture of Vimy Ridge was a triumph for Canadian forces and stressed that it was a great moment in the creation of the Canadian nation. "Every nation has a creation story to tell", he said. "The First World War and the battle of Vimy Ridge are central to the story of our country." Canadians had paid a heavy price for that victory. In an unfortunate choice of words, which left his meaning hovering uneasily between praise and condemnation, he told the living that they had an obligation to remember the "enormity" of that sacrifice and the "enormity" of their own duty, which was "to follow their example and to love our country and defend its freedom for ever". And he urged his audience, both there and the much larger one in Canada, to listen to the voices of the dead. "We may hear them say softly: I love my family, I love my comrades, I love my country, and I will defend their freedom to the end."

In Canada not everyone will agree with Harper's interpretation of what Vimy means for today. We have a multiplicity of views about the past and its significance for the present. In China, by contrast, the Communist Party does its best to ensure that the public gets only one version of history. When my book on Nixon's trip to China in 1972 came out, Chinese publishers showed an interest in translating it. There would, however, have to be a few small changes. Mention of the Cultural Revolution and of Mao's often scandalous private life would have to go. (The book has not been published in China.) Although the Communist Party has repudiated most of Mao's policies, it still holds him up as the father of the Communist Revolution. To question him would be to undermine the Party's own authority to rule China.

Authoritarian regimes also find a judicious use of the past a useful means of social control. In the 1990s, when the Chinese Communist Party grew concerned about the waning of Communist ideology and the demands for greater democracy, which had led to the demonstrations in Tiananmen Square in 1989, they called in Chinese history. In 1994, a member of the politburo, the central body of the Party, attended a memorial for the Yellow Emperor, a probably mythical figure from five thousand years ago who was said to be the father of all ethnic Chinese. It looked suspiciously like ancestor worship, one of the many traditional practices the Communists had condemned. The following year the authorities allowed a major conference on Confucius. Twenty years earlier, under the approving eyes of Mao, Red Guards had burned the great Confucian classics and done their best to destroy the sage's tomb. The Party also sponsored a major campaign for Patriotic Education, which emphasised, as the official directive put it, "the Chinese people's patriotism and brave patriotic deeds". The Great Wall, which had in previous decades been condemned for its cost in ordinary Chinese lives, now became the symbol of the Chinese will to survive and triumph. Very little was said about the joys of socialism, but China's past achievements were neatly linked to Communist Party rule: "Patriotism is a historical concept, which has different specific connotations in different stages and periods of social development. In contemporary China, patriotism is in essence identical to socialism." In other words, being loyal to China means being loyal to the Party. Chinese history was presented as the story of the centuries-old struggle of the Chinese people to unite and to progress in the face of determined interference and oppression from outside. China's failure to get the 2000 Olympic Games, the Opium Wars of the early nineteenth century, foreigners condemning the brutal crackdown in Tiananmen Square, and the Japanese invasion in the twentieth century were all wrapped up into one uninterrupted imperialist design to destroy the Chinese nation.

It is all too easy to rummage through the past and find nothing but a list of grievances, and many countries and peoples have done it. In the 1970s, Latin American nationalists blamed all their present problems on colonialism. The Chinese dwell on their Century of Humiliation and the ills they suffered at the hands of the imperialists. When the new state of Yugoslavia was formed after World War I, Serbs and Croats remembered quite different histories. Where the Serbs saw themselves as liberating their fellow southern Slavs, the Croats' history was rather one where they had been dragged unwillingly into a Serb-dominated country and denied a fair share in their own government.

French-Canadian nationalists have depicted a past in which the conquest by the British in 1763 led to two and a half centuries of humiliation. They play down or ignore the many and repeated examples of cooperation and friendship between French and English Canadians. French Canadians – innocent, benevolent, communitarian, and tolerant of others – are the heroes of the story; the English – coldhearted, passionless, and moneygrubbing – the villains. Esther Delisle, a Quebec historian, has run into trouble by attempting to show some ambiguities in that picture. She argues that Abbé Lionel Groulx, the renowned scholar and teacher, has become an icon to French-Canadian nationalists who manage, however, to overlook his anti-Semitism. While the nationalists stress the wrongs done to Quebec in the conscription crises of the two world wars, she points out that they fail to deal with the fact that in Quebec during World War II, there was considerable sympathy for the pro-Nazi Vichy government of France. As recent works on Pierre Trudeau confirm, he, like other members of the young French elite, carried on his life and career between 1939 and 1945 without paying much attention to what was going on in the world. "Reading the memoirs", writes Delisle, "of Pierre Elliott Trudeau, Gérard Pelletier and Gérard Filion, among other French Canadians promised to prestigious careers, one could conclude that they saw nothing, heard nothing, and said nothing at the time, and that they were only interested in (and marginally, at that) the struggle against conscription . . . There is more to the silence and lies than a simple narcissistic scratch. There is the need to hide positions which the Allied victory made unspeakable. These men would have to forget, and make others forget, their attraction to the siren songs of fascism and dictatorship in the worst cases, and in the best, their lack of opposition to them."

Stories of past glories or of past wrongs are useful tools in the present, but they, too, often come at the cost of abusing history. History is also abused when people try to ignore or even suppress evidence that might challenge their preferred view of the past. In Japan at present, the nationalist right is furious with archaeologists who are going to examine some of the scattered tombs where generations of the Japanese royal family are buried. Scholars have been asking for years for the right to investigate the sites, some of which go back to the third or fourth century. The nationalist fury grows out of their belief that the emperor is sacred and is, moreover, descended in an unbroken line from the sun. Japan, in the nationalist view, is a "divine land". The more prosaic explanation is that the royal family came originally from China or Korea; even if that is not true, it is probable that there was a good deal of intermarriage between Japan and the mainland so that the imperial family's bloodline may contain non-Japanese genes. If the investigations find evidence to confirm that hypothesis, a key part of the nationalists' mythology is destroyed.

The treatment of the sites has fluctuated with prevailing political currents. While the emperors were mere figureheads, most of the sites were neglected. With the Meiji Restoration in the second half of the nineteenth century, when Japan began its great national project of rapid modernisation, the emperor served as a convenient symbol of the national will, and a nationalist cult grew up around him. When suspected imperial tombs were discovered, the government bought the land and moved its owners away. No excavations were allowed until Japan's defeat in 1945. The American occupiers embarked on an ambitious program to remake Japanese society, and that included rewriting Japan's history. In theory, the ban on excavations of the imperial tombs was lifted, and indeed a number of discoveries were made which pointed to the extensive influence from both China and Korea on early Japanese culture. Access remains difficult, however, because the Imperial Household Agency, which runs the imperial properties, continues to insist that the sites are religious and that the spirits of the emperors' ancestors ought not to be disturbed. Archaeologists continue to demand that the agency allow fuller access. Several have received death threats from extreme nationalist groups.

Concern about what investigation of the past might reveal is by no means confined to Japan. In 1992 when a couple of spectators at hydroplane races on the Columbia River near Kennewick in the state of Washington stumbled on a human skull, their discovery set off a decade-long tug-of-war over the skull itself and the accompanying bones which were subsequently discovered. The remains turned out to be prehistoric, approximately nine thousand years old. Interestingly, the features of the skull appeared to be Caucasoid rather than aboriginal. These findings challenged what had until then been the widely accepted view that aboriginals were the first and only indigenous inhabitants of the Americas. The federal government, which would have preferred to avoid dealing with the issues raised, was prepared to hand over the bones to Native American tribes, but scientists sued for the right to do research. The Umatilla tribe argued that, according to its own myths, it had been near Kennewick since the beginning of time. "I have oral histories within my tribe that go back ten thousand years", said one member. "I know where my people lived, where they died, where they hunted, where they fished and where they were buried, because my oral histories tell me that." Kennewick man was an ancestor and must be properly buried. Furthermore, by letting the bones be investigated by scientists, the U.S. government was showing contempt for the tribe's sacred beliefs. After an eight-year legal battle, the courts ruled that the bones stay in the possession of the Army Corps of Engineers, on whose land they were found, and that scientists be given access.

History that challenges comfortable assumptions about a group is painful, but it is, as Michael Howard said, a mark of maturity. In recent years, Ireland has witnessed a major revision of its history in part because it is prosperous, successful, and self-confident and the old stories of victimhood no longer have the resonance they once did. As a result, the old, simple picture of Irish Catholic nationalists versus the Ulster Protestants and their English supporters and the two separate histories that each had is now being amended to show a more complex history, and some cherished myths are being destroyed. In World War I, it used to be believed, only the Protestants fought. The nationalists were engaged, depending on which way you looked at it, either in treason or in a struggle for liberty. In fact, 210,000 volunteers from Ireland, a majority of them Catholics and Irish nationalists, fought for the British against the Germans. The Easter Rising was not the unified movement of all Irish patriots of nationalist myth but the result, at least in part, of internal power struggles. As the president of Ireland, Mary McAleese, said in a recent lecture in London, "Where previously our history has been characterised by a plundering of the past for things to separate and differentiate us from one [another], our future now holds the optimistic possibility that Ireland will become a better place, where we will not only develop new relationships but will more comfortably revisit the past and find there . . . elements of kinship long neglected, of connections deliberately overlooked".

Distorted history, suppressed evidence – there is worse still, and that is the history that is simply false. Sometimes it is done for the best of motives, to build pride among those who have suffered much and who live with a deep sense of powerlessness and humiliation. In 1923, Marcus Garvey, the black American leader, wrote a stirring polemic titled "Who and What Is a Negro?" He tried to give his people back what slavery had stolen from them – a past as other peoples had, with a sense of who they were and what their achievements had been. He went further, though, and made claims which could not be substantiated. "Every student of history", he said, "of impartial mind, knows that the Negro once ruled the world, when white men were savages and barbarians living in caves; that thousands of Negro professors at that time taught in the universities in Alexandria, then the seat of learning; that ancient Egypt gave the world civilisation and that Greece and Rome have robbed Egypt of her arts and letters, and taken all the credit to themselves". His argument, which still keeps surfacing, was that civilisation was like a torch which had passed from sub-Saharan Africa to Egypt, then, in an act of theft, on to Greece and Rome. It is a curious and static view of civilisation as something that can be moved from one people to another – or that there is only one "civilisation." In reality, there are and have been many civilisations, and they are fluid and changing. The forces that shape them come from within and without. Of course, Greek civilisation had outside influences, but they were as likely to come from the East as from Egypt. And there is little evidence that Egyptian civilisation was derived largely from south of the Sahara.

More recent scholars have tried to bolster the claim by using linguistic and archaeological evidence. "Athens", it is claimed, is originally an African word, and Socrates was black because one sculpture shows him with a flat nose. Scholars in the field have dismissed such evidence, but for some of the more committed supporters of the Garvey thesis that is simply proof that Europeans ever since the Greeks have been engaged in a massive conspiracy to conceal their theft and the fact that they could not create civilisation on their own. According to Cheikh Anta Diop from Senegal, the Europeans even laid a trail of false evidence down through the centuries. Such stories bear the same relationship to the past as *The Da Vinci Code* does to Christian theology. They may help for a time to instill pride, but at a cost.

In India in the 1990s, the growth of Hindu nationalism

brought extraordinary attempts to eliminate parts of India's heritage and to rewrite Indian history. In 1992, fundamentalists, supported by right-wing Hindu politicians, destroyed a sixteenth-century mosque at Ayodhya in northern India on the grounds that it was built over the birthplace of the Hindu god Rama. Encouraged, they declared that they would move on to destroy other Muslim sites, including the Taj Mahal. This was part of a larger drive to peg India's identity as exclusively Hindu or, in the word used by the Hindu nationalists, "Hindutva."

India's history inevitably became a key component of this. The standard view, based on the evidence available, had been that the fertile Indus valley had housed the Harappan civilisation between about 3000 and 1700 B.C. It was gradually absorbed or disappeared when horse-borne Aryans moved down from the north, perhaps as peaceful migrants or possibly as warlike invaders. This did not suit the Hindu nationalists, because it implied that an indigenous civilisation had given way to one from outside and that their own culture might have foreign elements. As Madhav Golwalkar, the spiritual father of today's Hindu nationalists, wrote in the 1930s, "The Hindus came into this land from nowhere, but are indigenous children of the soil always, from times immemorial". Of course, this was an absurdly simplistic view of the ways peoples and civilisations develop and commingle. They are not flies stuck forever the same in amber but much more like rivers with many tributaries.

When the Hindu nationalist party, the Bharatiya Janata Party, won power at the centre in 1998, it immediately set to bringing the past into line with its views. Harappan civilisation was, it declared, actually Aryan. A terracotta seal from a Harappan site had been found which showed a horse. (This conclusive piece of evidence, unfortunately, turned out to be a fake.) Harappan civilisation was also, the government confidently pronounced, much older than previously accepted. Indeed, Murli Manohar Joshi, the BJP minister in charge of education between 1998 and 2004, announced that he had discovered an even older indigenous Indian civilisation, which he and his supporters named the Sarasvati. "The evidence for this", said Romila Thapar, one of India's most respected historians, "is so far invisible". Nevertheless, it was quite clear, at least to the BJP and its supporters, that India had housed the world's first civilisation. Not only had it been responsible for all manner of inventions and advances long before all others, but it had civilised the rest of the world. The Chinese may have been startled to learn that they were in fact also the descendants of Hindu warriors. Sanskrit, the ancient Indian language, was, it was claimed by the Hindu nationalists, the mother of all other languages. The Vedas, the oldest texts written in Sanskrit, were the foundation of most modern knowledge, including all of mathematics.

To make sure that Indian students absorbed all this, Joshi introduced new textbooks, which stressed such "Indian" subjects as yoga, Sanskrit, astrology, Vedic mathematics, and Vedic culture. He packed school boards and research centres with Hindu nationalists whose credentials as historians mattered far less than their adherence to a simplistic view of India's past and culture. The respected Indian Council of Historical Research in Delhi was told that its historian for early India was to be replaced by an engineer. That appointment at least did not go through, because there was a public outcry about both the appointee's credentials and his attacks on Christians and Muslims.

Behind these often laughable attempts to remake Indian education lay a more sinister and political agenda. The BJP and its supporters conceived of India as a Hindu nation and, moreover, one that reflected the values of upper-caste Hindus, including their reverence for cows and their hostility to beef eating. Their

India had little room or tolerance for the large religious minorities of Muslims and Christians, and precious little for lower-caste Hindus. The BJP view of the past was one in which Indian civilisation had been, from its inception, as Hindu as they were today. Even the merest suggestion that ancient Hindus had been different, that they might have eaten beef, for example, had to be taken out of the record. It was true, one Hindu nationalist admitted, that the evidence suggested that upper-caste Hindus ate beef in ancient times, but to let schoolchildren know that would confuse them and quite possibly traumatise them.

The BJP's India was one where Hindus had lived in harmony with one another until outsiders – Muslims and then the British – had arrived to damage and divide up Indian society through pillage, plunder and forcible conversions. The new textbooks dwelled on the sins of the outsiders but were largely silent on the often brutal deeds of Hindu rulers. Moreover, the texts ignored the copious evidence that down through the centuries, Muslims, Hindus, Christians and Sikhs – indeed, adherents of all religions – had for the most part lived peaceably side by side, borrowing and learning from one another. While Muslim invaders had brought Mogul and Persian styles in the arts into India, those had been absorbed and influenced by those already existing in India. The great Mogul emperor Akbar had been fascinated by other religions and had tried, unsuccessfully, to found a syncretic religion which incorporated elements of Islam, Hinduism and Christianity. In independent India, Jawaharlal Nehru, the first prime minister, had stood firmly for secularism and tolerance in a multi-ethnic, multi-faith India. None of this appeared in the Hindutva version of India's past. Rather, Muslims had always been enemies of Hindus and always would be until they were converted or otherwise dealt with.

Historians who pointed out the manifest flaws in this picture of India's past were condemned as Marxists or simply as bad Indians. It was a pity, said one fundamentalist, that there was no fatwa in Hinduism. In fact, extreme Hindu nationalists behaved as though there were. Scholars, including Romila Thapar, who published work that was at variance with the Hindutva orthodoxy received hate mail and even death threats. Expatriates, as is so often the case, were particularly vociferous in their defence of what they claimed was India's true history and culture. Thapar was hounded when she gave lectures in the United States. At a lecture in London, a Hindu activist threw an egg at Professor Wendy Doniger because she was daring to lecture on the great Hindu epic the *Ramayana*. In California, Hindu parents appeared before the state school board to demand that textbooks be purged of the errors propounded by "India-bashers" such as Thapar and scholars such as Michael Witzel of Harvard University. The errors they listed included, not surprisingly, the Aryan movement into India.

In a particularly bizarre series of incidents, James Laine, an American scholar at a small college in Minnesota who wrote a book investigating the myths surrounding the life of the seventeenth-century Hindu king and hero Shivaji, found himself the target of nationalist rage. Laine had dared to suggest that among the many stories was one that could be taken as a joking comment that Shivaji may not have been his father's son. The Shiv Sena, a right-wing political movement in Shivaji's home province of Maharashtra, ran a successful campaign to get Oxford University Press to withdraw the book. Early in 2004, a gang of toughs beat up and tarred a venerable Indian scholar whose name was mentioned in Laine's acknowledgments. Another mob broke into a research institute in Pune where Laine had done some work and, ironically, destroyed ancient Hindu writings and paintings and smashed a statue of the Hindu goddess of learning. The Pune police force responded by charging Laine and Oxford University Press with "wantonly giving provocation with intent to cause a riot". Indian moderate opinion was outraged and warned against the "Talibanisation" of India.

The impetus behind the attacks was, of course, as much about the present as it was about the past. It reflected competing views of Indian society – the Hindu versus the secular – and attempts by the politicians to appeal to Hindu nationalist sentiment. India was due to have a general election in the spring of 2004, and the Laine book became part of the campaign as politicians competed to show how Hindu and how Indian they were. There were calls for Interpol to arrest Laine. The BJP prime minister, Atal Behari Vajpayee, said foreign writers must learn that they could not offend Indian pride.

5

HISTORY AND NATIONALISM

Of the many ways in which we can define ourselves, the nation, at least for the last two centuries, has been one of the most enticing. The idea that we are part of a very large family, or, in Benedict Anderson's words, an imagined community, has been as powerful a force as Fascism or Communism. Nationalism brought Germany and Italy into being, destroyed Austria-Hungary, and, more recently, broke apart Yugoslavia. People have suffered and died, and have harmed and killed others, for their "nation."

History provides much of the fuel for nationalism. It creates the collective memories that help to bring the nation into being. The shared celebration of the nation's great achievements – and the shared sorrow at its defeats – sustain and foster it. The further back the history appears to go, the more solid and enduring the nation seems – and the worthier its claims. Ernest Renan, the nineteenth-century French thinker who wrote an early classic on nationalism, dismissed all the other justifications for the existence of nations, such as blood, geography, language or religion. "A nation", he wrote, "is a great solidarity created by the sentiment of the sacrifices which have been made and those which one is disposed to make in the future". As one of his critics preferred to put it, "A nation is a group of people united by a mistaken view about the past and a hatred of their neighbours." Renan saw the nation as something that depended on the assent of its members. "The existence of a nation is a plebiscite of every day, as the existence of an individual is a perpetual affirmation of life." For many nationalists, there is no such thing as voluntary assent; you were born into a nation and had no choice about whether or not you belonged, even if history had intervened. When France claimed the Rhineland after World War I, one of the arguments it used was that, even though they spoke German, its inhabitants were really French. Although ill fortune had allowed them to fall under German rule, they had remained French in essence, as their love of wine, their Catholicism, and their *joie de vivre* so clearly demonstrated.

Renan was trying to grapple with a new phenomenon because nationalism is a very late development indeed in terms of human history. For many centuries, most Europeans thought of themselves not as British (or English or Scottish or Welsh), French, or German but as members of a particular family, clan, region, religion or guild. Sometimes they defined themselves in terms of their overlords, whether local barons or emperors. When they did define themselves as German or French, it was as much a cultural category as a political one, and they certainly did not assume, as modern national movements almost always do, that nations had a right to rule themselves on a specific piece of territory.

Those older ways of defining oneself persisted well into the modern age. When commissions from the League of Nations tried to determine borders after World War I in the center of Europe, they repeatedly came upon locals who had no idea whether they were Czechs or Slovaks, Lithuanians or Poles. We are Catholic or Orthodox, came the answers, merchants or farmers, or simply people of this village or that. Danilo Dolci, the Italian sociologist and activist, was astonished to find in the 1950s that there were people living in the interior of Sicily who had never heard of Italy, even though, in theory, they had been Italians for several generations. They were the anomalies, though, left behind as nationalism increasingly became the way in which Europeans defined themselves. Rapid communications, growing literacy, urbanisation, and above all the idea that it was right and proper to see oneself as part of a nation, and a nation, moreover, which ought to have its own state on its own territory, all fed into the great wave of nationalism which shook Europe in the nineteenth century and the wider world in the twentieth.

For all the talk about eternal nations, they are created not by fate or God but by the activities of human beings, and not least by historians. It all started so quietly in the nineteenth century. Scholars worked on languages, classifying them into different families and trying to determine how far back into history they went. They discovered rules to explain changes in language and were able to establish, at least to their own satisfaction, that texts centuries old were written in early forms of, for example, German or French. Ethnographers like the Grimm brothers collected German folk tales as a way of showing that there was something called the German nation in the Middle Ages. Historians worked assiduously to recover old stories and pieced together the history of what they chose to call their nation as though it had an unbroken existence since antiquity. Archaeologists claimed to have found evidence that showed where such nations had once lived, and where they had moved to during the great waves of migrations.

The cumulative result was to create an unreal yet influential version of how nations formed. While it could not be denied that different peoples, from Goths to Slavs, had moved into and across Europe, mingling as they did so with peoples already there, such a view assumed that at some point, generally in the Middle Ages, the music had stopped. The dancing pieces had fallen into their chairs, one for the French, another for the Germans and yet another for the Poles. And there history had fixed them as "nations." German historians, for example, could depict an ancient German nation whose ancestors had lived happily in their forests from before the time of the Roman Empire and which at some time, probably in the first century A.D., had become recognisably "German." So – and this was the dangerous question – what was properly the German nation's land? Or the land of any other "nation"? Was it where the people now lived, where they had lived at the time of their emergence in history, or both?

Would the scholars have gone on with their speculations if they could have seen what they were preparing the way for? The bloody wars that created Italy and Germany? The passions and hatred that tore apart the old multinational Austria-Hungary? The claims, on historical grounds, by new and old nations after World War I for the same pieces of territory? The hideous regimes of Hitler and Mussolini with their elevation of the nation and the race to the supreme good and their breathtaking demands for the lands of others?

A paradox, as the British historian Eric Hobsbawm put it, is that "nationalism is modern but it invents for itself history and traditions". The histories that fed and still feed into nationalism draw on what already exists rather than inventing new facts. They often contain much that is true, but they are slanted to confirm the existence of the nation through time, and to encourage the hope that it will continue. They help to create symbols of victory or defeat – Waterloo, Dunkirk, Stalingrad, Gettysburg, or, for Canadians, Vimy Ridge. They highlight the deeds of past leaders – Charles Martel defeating the Moors at Tours; Elizabeth I at Plymouth Hoe facing the Spanish Armada; Horatio Nelson destroying the French fleet at Trafalgar; George Washington refusing to lie about his cherry tree. Often nationalism borrows from the trappings of religious identity. Think of the war memorials that resemble martyrs or Christ on the cross, or the elaborate rituals on days such as November 11.

Many of what the present age thinks of as age-old symbols and ceremonies are often newly minted, as each generation looks through the past and finds what suits its present needs. In 1953, all around the world those who had televisions watched, with awe and fascination, the ancient coronation rituals – the monarch's ride through London in the gilded state coach, the solemn procession into Westminster Abbey, the music, the decorations, the archbishop of Canterbury in his magnificent robes, the elaborate ceremony of crowning. As a schoolchild in Canada, I was given a booklet that explained it all. What most of us did not know was that much of what we watched with such respect was a creation of the nineteenth century. Earlier coronations had been slipshod, even embarrassing affairs. When a hugely fat George IV was crowned in 1820, his estranged queen, Caroline, hammered on the door. At Queen Victoria's coronation in 1837, the clergy stumbled through the service, and the archbishop of Canterbury had trouble with the ring, which was much too big for her finger. By the end of the century, the monarchy was more important as the symbol of a much more powerful Britain. Royal occasions became grander and were much better rehearsed. New ones were added: David Lloyd George, the radical prime minister from Wales, found it useful to have a formal ceremony within the ancient walls of Caernarfon Castle to install the later Edward VIII as Prince of Wales.

One of the most famous of national symbols is the Battle of Kosovo, where Serbian forces were defeated by the Ottoman Turks in 1389. In Serbian nationalist lore, this was both an earthly and a spiritual defeat that contains within it, however, the promise of resurrection. For Serbian nationalists, the story is tragically clear. The Christian Serbs were defeated, through treachery, by the Muslim Ottomans. The night before the battle, Prince Lazar, the Serbian leader, had a vision in which he was promised that he could have either the kingdom of heaven or one on earth. A good Christian, he chose the former, but the implicit promise was that one day the Serbian nation would be resurrected on earth. Spiritual salvation or earthly? Lazar died on the battlefield, after he was betrayed by a Judas, a fellow Serb. His people, true to their faith, remembered the defeat and the promise and longed for a restored Serbian state for the next four hundred years.

The only problem with the story is that not only is it much too simple but parts of it are not supported by the sketchy records from the time. Prince Lazar was not the ruler of all the Serbs but merely one among the several princes who were scrambling for power in the wreckage of the Serbian empire built by Prince Dusan. Some had already made their peace with the Ottomans and as vassals of the sultan had sent troops to fight against Lazar. It is not clear that the battle was an overwhelming defeat for the Serbs; at the time, reports in fact called it a victory. It may equally as well have been a draw because neither side resumed hostilities for a time. And an independent Serbian state lingered on for decades.

Lazar's widow and Orthodox monks began the process of turning the dead prince into a martyr for the Serbs, curiously at the same time as his son was fighting as a vassal for the Turks. For centuries, though, Lazar and Kosovo were symbols more of Serbs as Orthodox Christians and a people who had a common language than of an independent Serbian nation-state. The story was kept alive in the monasteries, along with much other Serbian culture, and in the great epic poems which were passed down through the generations. It was only in the nineteenth century, with the awakening of nationalism throughout Europe, that that story became so central in mobilising Serbs to fight for independence against a declining and incompetent Ottoman Empire.

In the first half of the nineteenth century, with history as their inspiration, the Serbs moved toward first autonomy within the Ottoman Empire and then full independence. The highly influential Serbian scholar of the early nineteenth century Vuk Karadžić standardised a modern Serbian written language and collected the epic poems. He also left a poisoned legacy by arguing that those peoples such as Croats and Bosnian Muslims who spoke virtually the same language were also Serbs. Ilija Garašanin, the statesman who did so much to shape Serbian nationalism and to build the structures for the new Serbian state, drew on history to point his fellow Serbs toward their destiny. The Serbian Empire had been destroyed by the Ottoman Turks, but now the time had come to restore it. We are, he said in a document that remained secret until the start of the twentieth century, the "true heirs of our great forefathers". Serbian nationalism was not something new or, heaven forbid, revolutionary but the flowering of ancient roots. Again, it was a dangerous vision because it assumed that the Croats and Bosnians were a natural part of the empire.

It is easy to challenge such views of the past but not to shake the faith of those who wish to believe in them. In the break-up of Yugoslavia in the 1980s and 1990s, the old historical myths came to the forefront again. Yet again, the Serbs were fighting on alone in a hostile world. In 1986, a memorandum from the Serbian

Academy of Sciences warned that all the gains the Serbs had made since they first rebelled against the Ottomans in 1804 were going to be lost. Croats were terrorising the Serbs in Croatia, and Albanians were forcing Serbs to flee the province of Kosovo. In 1989, Slobodan Milošević went to Kosovo on the six-hundredth anniversary of the battle and declared, "The Kosovo heroism does not allow us to forget that, at one time, we were brave and dignified and one of the few who went into battle undefeated". At the same time, in Croatia, nationalists were looking back into their past to argue that a greater Croatia, incorporating hundreds of thousands of Serbs, was historically necessary. History did not destroy Yugoslavia or lead to the horrors that accompanied that destruction, but its skilful manipulation by men such as Milošević and, in Croatia, Franjo Tudjman helped to mobilise their followers and intimidate the uncommitted.

The Balkans have had, in Winston Churchill's marvellous phrase, more history than they can consume. New nations have worried that they do not have enough. When Israel came into existence in 1948, it was, despite the long connection of Jews with Palestine, a new state. With immigrants from all over Europe, and, increasingly, by the 1950s from the Middle East, building a strong national identity was essential if Israel itself were to survive. It was difficult to identify shared customs and culture. What did a Jew from Egypt have in common with one from Poland? Nor was religion a sufficient basis; many Zionists were resolutely non-religious. Although Hebrew was reviving, it had not yet produced a national literature. That gave history particular significance as a glue. In its Declaration of Independence, Israel called on the past to justify its existence. The land was the historic birthplace of the Jewish people: "After being forcibly exiled from their land, the people kept faith with it throughout their Dispersion and never ceased to pray and hope for their return to it and for the restoration of their political freedom." More recent history became part of the story, too. The Jews had managed to return in great numbers: "They made deserts bloom, revived the Hebrew language, built villages and towns, and created a thriving community, controlling its own economy and culture, loving peace but knowing how to defend itself, bringing the blessings of progress to all the country's inhabitants, and aspiring towards independent nationhood."

In 1953, the Israeli Knesset passed the State Education Law and a law (Yad Vashem) to commemorate the Holocaust. The laws' author was the minister of education and culture, Ben-Zion Dinur, who had been active as a Zionist educator and politician long before Israel's independence. His view of history was rooted in the need to build an Israeli consciousness. "The ego of a nation", he declared in the Knesset, "exists only to the extent that it has a memory, to the extent that the nation knows how to combine its past experiences into a single entity". For Dinur and those who supported him (and many on both the Left and the Right did not), that meant teaching Israelis that there was and always had been an Israeli nation, that it had survived the long centuries of exile, and that it had always been focused on getting back to its lost lands. Israel therefore was the heir and the culmination of a long historical process. Dinur's view has been much criticised for leaving out religion, for example, in the definition of Jewishness and for presenting an oversimplified view of Jewish history, but it has been very influential in Israeli schools. A study of textbooks used between 1900 and 1984 found that increasingly as time went on, Jewish history was presented in terms of the establishment of Israel, that among Jews in exile the Zionist dream of a Jewish state was "the strongest and oldest" movement.

Nationalism has far from run its course, and new nations keep appearing – and they, too, find history important in defining themselves. In the 1960s, Wolfgang Feuerstein, a young German scholar, came upon a people inhabiting a remote valley on the south coast of the Black Sea near the Turkish port of Trabzon. The approximately 250,000 Lazi were Muslim, like the great majority of Turks, but had their own language, customs and myths. It seemed to the young German that they must have once been Christian. He started to study them, this anomaly left behind by history, and, to help record their stories, he devised a written language for them. The Lazi began to take an interest in their own past and culture, and the Turkish authorities, who have enough trouble with the demands of their other minorities, such as the Kurds, became concerned. Feuerstein was arrested, beaten, and deported, but from his exile he has sent texts with Lazi stories and poetry back to the unofficial schools which are now being run surreptitiously. As the Lazi develop a sense of themselves and their past, they are becoming a nation. In 1999, a Laz Party was established to push for a "Lazistan" within Turkey. Its manifesto talks of fostering the Laz language and culture and encouraging the study of history from a Laz point of view. And, if I am not mistaken, they will use that history to present a bill of claims one day.

6

PRESENTING
HISTORY'S BILL

Anyone who has ever had an argument and said, "You always do that" or "I trusted you" or "You owe me one", is using history to gain an advantage in the present. And almost all of us, from heads of countries to private citizens, do it. We spin the events of the past to show that we always tend to behave well and our opponents badly or that we are normally right and others wrong. Therefore, it goes almost without saying, we are in the right again this time.

When the troubles started in Yugoslavia in the 1990s, all sides called on history to justify what they were doing. The Serbs portrayed themselves as the historic defenders of Christianity against the Muslim onslaught and as the liberators of other southern Slavs such as the Croats and the Slovenes. The Croats saw a very different past. Croatia had always been part of the West, of the great Austrian Empire, and of Catholic civilisation, while Serbia came out of the backward and superstitious world of Orthodoxy. The government in Serbia started to refer to Croats as Ustasha – the name of Fascist forces of World War II that had massacred Serbs and Jews. Serbian television repeatedly showed documentaries about the Ustasha, with the obvious implied warning that this could happen again. Croatia's president, Franjo Tudjman, like Milošević another Communist turned nationalist, responded with scorn. The Ustasha certainly had committed crimes, but it was nevertheless "an expression of the Croatian nation's historic desire for an independent homeland".

When Serbian forces started to attack Bosnian Muslims, they tried to justify their unprovoked aggression by telling the world that they were yet again defending the Christian West against the fanatical East. The fact that Bosnian Muslims were not only largely secular but mostly descended from Serbs or Croats was not allowed to stand in the way. Serbian nationalists insisted on referring to them as Turks or traitors to the Serbs and the Serbian Orthodox Church. Croatians, of course, preferred to see the Bosnian Muslims as apostate Croatian Catholics. (Ironically, the effect of the war has been to make many Muslims in Bosnia much more devout.)

Using history to label or diminish your opponents has always been a useful tool. The Left shouts "Fascist!" at the Right while conservatives throw around the Stalinist and Communist labels. When Ariel Sharon, then prime minister of Israel, visited New York in 2005, he faced protesters who shouted "Auschwitz" and "Nazi" because he had dismantled illegal Jewish settlements in the Gaza Strip. In January 2006, as Hillary Clinton was opening her campaign for the presidency, she attacked the House of Representatives, then dominated by the Republicans. "When you look at the way the House of Representatives has been run", she told a predominantly black audience in Harlem, "it has been run like a plantation and you know what I am talking about." They did, and so did the Republicans who accused her of trying to play the race card.

Countries also use episodes from the past to shame and put

pressure on others. China, for example, repeatedly refers to the Century of Humiliation, which started with the first Opium War in 1839 and ended with the triumph of the Communists in 1949. The Chinese have a long list of grievances: defeat at the hands of foreign powers, from Britain to Japan; the 1860 burning of the Summer Palace in Beijing by British and French troops; foreign concession areas where foreign nationals made fortunes and lived under their own laws; unequal treaties that undermined China's autonomy; and, of course, the famous "Dogs and Chinese Not Admitted" sign. When the United States sells weapons to Taiwan, China reminds it of American support for the Communists' enemies in the past. When Henry Kissinger made his first secret trip to China in the summer of 1972, he had to sit through repeated reminders by the then prime minister, Zhou Enlai, of past American sins, including the famous occasion at the Geneva conference in 1954 when John Foster Dulles, the secretary of state, refused to shake Zhou's hand. In 1981, China's then leader, Deng Xiaoping, complained to the United States about its reluctance to sell China advanced technology: "Perhaps the problem is one of how the U.S. treats China. I wonder whether the U.S. is still not treating China as a hostile country".

In the Chinese Communist Party's history, China is the eternal victim, and so it can do no wrong. It has been a peaceful power throughout its long history, never trying to conquer other peoples or grab territory, unlike the Western powers or Japan. When China receives worldwide criticism for its support of dreadful regimes like the ones in Burma and Sudan, yet again it is being unfairly treated. Foreign powers, in the Chinese view, cynically use talk of human rights abuses to attack China and to interfere in its internal affairs. The Dalai Lama, supported by wicked and self-serving forces in the West, puts out false stories about Tibet when, according to the official Chinese line, what had been a backward and priest-ridden society is rapidly modernising with China's unstinting help. In any case, say the Chinese, Westerners have no moral authority to criticise them when the West's own history includes imperialism, slavery and the Holocaust. When the Canadian government recently made enquiries about the fate of the Canadian citizen Huseyin Celil, who is being held in a Chinese prison, the Chinese countered with charges that, yet again, foreigners were trying to humiliate China but that China would stand firm. An interesting variant on the use of history to justify present-day behaviour surfaced during the 2008 summer Olympics. When foreign critics pointed out that the Chinese authorities were not, as they had apparently promised the International Olympic Committee, respecting human rights, the response by China's defenders was that foreigners had no authority to criticise China since they did not know its long history.

In its relations with Japan, China has made great use of the past, in particular the Japanese invasion and occupation between 1937 and 1945 and the well-documented atrocities, such as the rape of Nanjing by Japanese troops, which accompanied it. Japan's behavior in China and its role in provoking World War II in Asia have been the subjects of painful debate within Japan, but the Chinese government has chosen to believe that Japan continues to deny its culpability. In the 1990s, as the Communist Party started the Patriotic Education campaign to bolster its own authority, attacks on Japan and its reputed amnesia grew. Painting modern Japan as the unrepentant successor to the militaristic country of World War II was a convenient way of justifying China's own claims to leadership in Asia and undermining Japan's claims for a seat on an expanded UN Security Council. In the spring of 2005, under the benevolent eye of the authorities, and perhaps with their direct encouragement, young Chinese attacked Japanese businesses in several of China's big cities on the grounds that Japanese textbooks were omitting all references to the sack of Nanjing. When the disturbances spread, however, and the targets widened to include the failings of the Chinese government in such areas as the environment, the Party decided enough was enough. The nationalist outbursts stopped. The emotions they were tapping into remain, though, and the Party continues to be tempted to play the dangerous game of using nationalism to bolster its declining ideological authority.

Sometimes the present is called in to effect changes in the past. To take one example which has been much in the news lately: Armenian groups around the world argue that Turkey should not be allowed into the European Union until it has admitted that it conducted genocide more than ninety years ago. It is absolutely true that a dreadful thing was done to the Armenian subjects of the Ottoman Turks during World War I. As Russian armies advanced on Turkey, the Turkish government feared that the Armenians would offer support to the invaders. Hundreds of thousands of Armenians were forcibly uprooted from their homes in the northeast of Turkey and sent south. Many did not survive the trek. They were harried by local Muslims, often Kurds, and the Turkish authorities either watched with indifference or actively encouraged the killing. In countries such as the United States, Canada and France, Armenians and their supporters have persuaded legislators to define the murders as genocide, arguing that it was official Turkish policy to exterminate the Armenians, and to demand that the Turkish government of today make a full apology. The Turks have dug in their heels, arguing that today's Turkey should not bear the responsibility for what was done in the past by a very different regime. They deny, moreover, that what occurred was genocide. The issue has further complicated the vexed question of Turkey's admission to the European Union.

In the aftermath of World War I, the Germans used history as a weapon in another way, to undermine the legitimacy of the Treaty of Versailles, which they had signed with the victorious Allies. Military defeat – and there is no doubt that it was that – came as a terrible shock to the German civilian government and to ordinary Germans, both of whom had been kept in the dark by the supreme command. From 1918 on, the army did its best to avoid responsibility for defeat by sedulously fostering the myth of the stab in the back: Germany had been defeated not on the battlefield but by the activities of traitors at home, whether socialists, pacifists, Jews or a combination of all three. The fact that the Allies decided, partly for reasons of their own war weariness, not to invade and occupy Germany (apart from a small slice on the west side of the Rhine) gave the myth more credibility among the German people. The sense that Germany ought not to be treated as a defeated nation was also enhanced by the circumstances of its surrender. Its government had exchanged notes with the American president, Woodrow Wilson, in which he had talked of a peace without recrimination or vengeance. As far as the Germans were concerned, the armistice with the Allies had been made on the basis of Wilson's Fourteen Points, which painted a picture of a new and peaceable world based on justice and respect for the rights of peoples. Surely that meant that the Allies would not seek to slice off great pieces of German territory, inhabited by Germans, or demand heavy reparations? In any event, to strengthen Germany's case for gentle treatment, the country argued that it was a different Germany. The kaiser had fled, and the monarchy had vanished. Germany was now a republic, and why should it pay for the sins of its predecessor? When Germans discovered the terms of the Treaty of Versailles in the spring of 1919, their reaction was one of shock and a conviction that they had been betrayed. And when they found out that there were to be no serious negotiations but merely a deadline for signing, they denounced the treaty as the *"Diktat"*.

In the 1920s, hostility to the treaty went right across the political spectrum within Germany. The terms were seen as punitive and illegitimate, and there was widespread if unspoken agreement that they should be circumvented wherever possible. What was particularly galling was Article 231, which assigned Germany responsibility for starting the war. The "war guilt" clause, as it came misleadingly to be known, was intended both to convey the Allies' moral disapprobation and, perhaps even more important, to provide a legal basis for demanding reparations. The leader of the German delegation which received the terms made a conscious decision to attack Article 231, and back in Germany the Foreign Ministry set up a special unit to continue his work. The events of July 1914 came in for particular scrutiny. Selected documents were released or shown to sympathetic historians to create a picture of a Europe stumbling toward war. The catastrophe was no one's and everyone's fault. Germany bore no more responsibility than any another country.

Within Germany, such views of the past were immensely influential in fuelling both a deep sense of grievance against the Allies (and indeed against the German government, largely made up of Socialists, which had signed the treaty) and a strong desire to burst the "chains" of the Versailles Treaty. As he started to gather support among disgruntled veterans, extreme right-wingers, and the floating population of the Munich beer halls in the early 1920s, Adolf Hitler hammered on the themes of the stab in the back and the unjust peace. As he gained a hearing among the respectable middle classes, it was that appeal to a frustrated German nationalism that helped him to gain legitimacy. Unfortunately for the peace of the world, the rewriting of history made an impact outside Germany as well, particularly in the English-speaking countries. Increasingly, the leaders and publics in countries such as the United Kingdom and the United States took the view that Germany had indeed been unfairly treated and that it was quite right to demand a revision of the Treaty of Versailles. The distortion and misuse of history served Hitler well in two ways: by bringing him supporters and by feeding the appeasement policies of his potential opponents.

In the past two centuries, history has become important in another way – as a basis for claiming land, both within countries and between them. This is partly because, where there are no clear records transferring land from one group of people to another, as is the case with much Native land in Canada, evidence of possession in the past helps to support arguments that the transfer was illegal. Furthermore, we no longer regard treaties and agreements signed when one side does not have the slightest idea of what the words mean as valid. When Henry Stanley travelled up the Congo River getting local chiefs to put their marks on what were to them meaningless bits of paper, he acquired for King Leopold of Belgium a vast territory. And the great powers acquiesced. They were, after all, doing much the same thing themselves. Today we would treat such sharp dealing as fraud.

Nor, unless we are religious fanatics, do we believe that promises from the gods are a sound basis for claiming territory. Other traditional grounds for claiming territory are equally unacceptable today. Marriage, for example. When Charles II of Britain married Catherine of Braganza, she brought Bombay with her as part of her dowry. Today if Prince Charles wished to give the Duchy of Cornwall to his new wife, it would be simply unthinkable. Monarchs no longer can swap pieces of territory as they did for so many centuries. Napoleon could sell a huge chunk of the New World to the United States in the 1803 Louisiana Purchase; President Nicolas Sarkozy would not be able to sell even the smallest piece of France – the islands of St Pierre and Miquelon, for example – today. At the Congress of Vienna, which ended the Napoleonic Wars, kingdoms, duchies, counties and cities were bartered among the powers in a great game of Monopoly, and no one saw anything wrong in it. A century later, at the conclusion of World War I, the Paris Peace Conference spent much time and effort trying to determine the wishes of the inhabitants – or at the very least their ethnicity – of the territories it found at its disposal.

Ways of thinking change, and what seemed perfectly normal two centuries ago now is literally unthinkable. War and conquest used to be quite standard ways of shifting boundaries about. If you lost a war, you could expect to give up money, art treasures, territory, weapons and anything else the victor demanded. The spread of ideas about popular sovereignty, democracy, citizenship and nationalism has meant that even the most ruthless of rulers had to pay at least lip service to the notion that peoples have a right to self-determination. When Hitler moved east into the Soviet Union, he claimed to be following the natural and historical path of the German race. When Stalin scooped Eastern Europe into his empire at the end of World War II, his cover story was that the Soviet Union was responding to the will of the local peoples or that it was simply restoring its historic boundaries. When Saddam Hussein occupied Kuwait in 1990, he tried to justify his actions with unconvincing references to Kuwait recognising Iraqi suzerainty in the eighteenth century, long, of course, before either country existed. History has become ever more necessary to provide legitimacy to claims to land as most other grounds, whether marriage or conquest, have fallen away.

After the Franco-Prussian War of 1870–71, which resulted in a humiliating defeat for France and the birth of the new Germany, the German generals insisted on claiming the two French provinces of Alsace and Lorraine, partly as spoils of war, partly to provide a defensive barrier against future French attacks. German nationalists obligingly cast their demands in newer, more acceptable clothes. In the past, Alsace and part of Lorraine had been part of the Holy Roman Empire and for much of their history had had German rulers. Louis XIV had seized Alsace and Louis XV Lorraine, but the time had come to restore them to their natural home. No matter if many of their inhabitants did not speak German or preferred to remain with France. Heinrich von Treitschke, one of Germany's leading historians, said the German nation knew what was best for "these unfortunates" who had so sadly fallen under French influence. "We shall restore them to their true selves against their will." A German newspaper recommended the nineteenth-century version of tough love. "We must begin with the rod", it declared. "Love will follow the disciplining, and it will make them Germans again."

In 1919, at the Paris Peace Conference, which marked the end of World War I, justification for claims to territory assumed huge importance because there was so much to be divided up and so many competing claims. The defeat of Germany, the collapse of Russia and the Russian Empire, and the disintegration of Austria-Hungary and of the Ottoman Empire meant that borders all over Europe and the Middle East were in a state of flux. Old nations, such as Poland, saw the chance to put themselves on the map again, and new ones, such as Czechoslovakia, had their chance to be born. Woodrow Wilson's speeches and the talk of self-determination that was in the air everywhere encouraged dozens of groups to make their way to Paris to lay their cases before the great powers.

Their arguments fell into three main categories: strategic, that possession of a particular piece of territory was necessary for a country's safety or for its economy; ethnographic, that the peoples on the ground belonged to the petitioning nation through language, customs, or religion; and finally, and this was often considered the clincher, by historical right. Strategic or economic arguments did not always work, because neighbouring countries could make the same case. Ethnography was also tricky where, as was the case in the centre of Europe, populations were so mixed. History seemed to speak with authority – or did it? Europe, and it is true of the Middle East as well, has far too much history, as Winston Churchill memorably quipped about the Balkans, more than it can consume. Empires and states, rulers and peoples, had come and gone. You could almost always find a basis for your claims in the past if you looked hard enough. Italy claimed much of the Dalmatian coast, partly to defend its own Adriatic coast, partly on the grounds that Italian civilisation was superior to that of the largely Slavic inhabitants, but also because Venice had once ruled it. And human nature being what it is, when the petitioners at the peace conference ransacked history, those who spoke for emerging nations did not go back to a time when their putative forerunners had occupied a small piece of territory. Many Poles, including Roman Dmowski, leader of the Polish delegation to Paris, wanted at least to re-establish the borders of 1772, when Poland ruled over today's Lithuania and Belarus and much of Ukraine. "When Dmowski related the claims of Poland", said an American expert, "he began at eleven o'clock in the morning and in the fourteenth century, and could reach the year 1919 and the pressing problems of the moment only as late as four o'clock in the afternoon". The Serbs longed for the boundaries of the fourteenth century, when King Stephen's kingdom stretched from the Aegean up to the Danube. The Bulgarians preferred the tenth-century map, when their king Simeon had ruled over much of the same territory.

"Each one of the Central European nationalities", the same American expert complained wearily, "had its own bagful of statistical and cartographical tricks. When statistics failed, use was made of maps in colour. It would take a huge monograph to contain an analysis of all the types of map forgeries that the war and the peace conference called forth". Or the abuses of history. The records of the conference are full of sweeping claims buttressed by shaky histories which skip lightly over the centuries, the coming and going of states, the unending movements of peoples across the face of Europe, and all other inconvenient facts, and which purport to show that such and such a piece of land was always Polish or Italian. When Serbia and Romania both claimed the Banat, which lies between them, for example, they reached back to the Middle Ages for evidence to support their claims. Look, said the Serbian representative, at the monasteries in the Banat, which had always been Serbian. That, replied the Romanian, was because Slavs were more naturally pious than Romanians.

Today, China uses history to recast its invasion and occupation of Tibet as not anything of the sort. In the view of the Chinese government, it simply reasserted its historical rights, which had been established over the centuries. Taiwan, at least to the Chinese, presents a similar case. As Zhou Enlai said to Henry Kissinger in 1972, "History also proves that Taiwan has belonged to China for more than a thousand years – a longer period than Long Island has been part of the U.S." In fact, history proves no such thing. In the case of Tibet, it is true that Dalai Lamas from time to time recognised the mandate of heaven of the emperor in far-off China, but for most of the time the remote mountain land was left to its own devices. Taiwan has had even looser ties with China. It was too far across the sea for most Chinese dynasties to bother with. Only the last dynasty, the Qing, tried to assert some control, partly because the island had become a refuge for pirates and rebels.

History takes on particular importance when land is under dispute. In Canada, aboriginals use printed records such as treaties and dispatches as well as oral histories and archaeology to claim back what they argue are their ancestral lands. Romanians claim, as they did in Paris in 1919, that the rich prize of Transylvania should be theirs because they are the descendants of Roman legions and therefore have been there much longer than their Hungarian opponents, who only arrived in the ninth century. Albanians claim that Kosovo is theirs because they are descendants of ancient Illyrians, who were known in classical Greek times, while the Serbs only came in the eleventh century. Serbs counter with the argument that most of the Albanians in Kosovo are new arrivals, part of the wave that came in the nineteenth and twentieth centuries.

In one of the most difficult and dangerous disputes in the present, Israelis and Palestinians argue over possession of the small piece of land that was once Palestine in the Ottoman Empire. Every aspect of their joint history is disputed. Did Palestine really have a population of 90 per cent Palestinian Arabs and 10 per cent Jews at the time of World War I? Did the Palestinians turn down chance after chance to cooperate with the Jews? Or did the Jews increasingly exclude them from the economy and from power? Is it really possible to speak of a "Palestinian people"? (Golda Meir and David Ben-Gurion both thought not.) Was 1948, when the state of Israel was proclaimed, a triumph or a catastrophe? Did the Palestinian refugees leave willingly because they thought they would be coming back with victorious Arab armies, or were they pushed out? Has a tiny Israel always been circled by an iron ring of implacable Arab enemies? Was its survival a miracle or because it had a lot of advantages on its side? Did the Palestinians support the Axis in World War II? Is Zionism another version of Western colonialism?

It is almost impossible for the two sides to find common answers to such questions because history lies at the heart of both their identity and their claims to Palestine. Israeli history was for a long time very much what the founding fathers such as Ben-Zion Dinur had hoped it would become – an inspiring story to weld Israelis into a nation determined to survive. Israel belongs in Palestine because there has been a continuous Jewish presence there since the Romans conquered the last independent Jewish state. The Arabs, the argument went, were relative newcomers, drifting in over the centuries from elsewhere. Moreover, so political figures like Golda Meir insisted, they did not constitute a separate nation called Palestinians. In the 1980s, an American writer named Joan Peters went still further, attempting to show, unsuccessfully, that there had been virtually no Arabs at all in Palestine when the Zionist settlers started to arrive at the end of the nineteenth century; attracted by the prosperity the Zionists were creating, so she claimed, they moved in. Modern Israel was born in adversity yet managed to triumph over its massed Arab enemies. In the years after 1948, it was attacked repeatedly by its neighbours and forced into three defensive wars, in 1956, 1967, and 1973. It hangs on to the occupied territories of Gaza, the West Bank, and the Golan Heights to ensure its safety. Israel, so this version says, would like peace, but the Arabs have been intransigent right from the start.

Palestinian and the wider Arab history is, not surprisingly, different. In their view of the past, the Jewish presence – the "usurping entity" – was planted in Palestine in the twentieth century by Western imperialism in a classic act of colonialism. Israel's birth was assisted by powerful midwives, especially the United States. The Palestinians, who have been a people for decades, if not centuries, resisted but were too weak, and their Arab brethren were divided and, in the case of Jordan and Egypt, colluding secretly with Israel to seize Palestinian land. The refugees did not leave willingly in 1948 but were forced out, often at gunpoint, by Jewish soldiers. It is Israel, with its massive support from the United States, that is the region's bully and warmonger. Israel refuses to hand back the land it seized in 1967, even though its occupation is illegitimate, and it treats the Palestinian inhabitants of the occupied territories in a way that resembles South African apartheid. The Palestinian leadership has tried to negotiate with Israel in good faith; if negotiations have failed, like the ones President Clinton sponsored at Camp David, it is Israel's fault.

Recent history is only part of the battleground and perhaps not even the most important. If the two sides can demonstrate that their peoples have a long-standing and unbroken connection to the land, then that, in the way pioneered by nationalist movements in Europe, becomes a title deed for the present. That is why the settler movement in Israel prefers to use the biblical names of Judaea and Samaria to describe the West Bank. As a spokeswoman for Gush Emunim, one of the more radical groups, put it, history was their "currency". Not surprisingly, as Nadia Abu El-Haj has pointed out in *Facts on the Ground*, archaeology has assumed a central importance in the dispute between Israelis and Palestinians because it promises definitive answers. If, for example, Iron Age sites can be shown to be those of the Israelites, who conquered the land of the Canaanites, then that might establish a modern Jewish claim to the same land. If, on the other hand, the sites were shared by various peoples at different times, an unbroken connection might be harder to establish. "It would not be right", said a Palestinian archaeologist, "to emphasise the history of one people among the many peoples who invaded Palestine and settled there". Or what if, as some Arab archaeologists argue, the original inhabitants were Arabs whose land was taken by the Israelites? Each century becomes part of the debate. If a tenth-century mosaic is Arab, what does it mean for the

Palestinian claims? "Do we have to tell the world this country was settled by Muslims?" an Israeli colonel once asked an archaeologist in exasperation.

When agreements were reached, with great difficulty in the early 1990s, for Israel to withdraw from parts of the West Bank, archaeological finds were part of the bargaining. The Palestinians demanded them back; the Israeli government insisted on joint management of important sites. Who owned antiquities in places such as Jericho, which were due to be handed over to the Palestinian National Authority? In 1993, the Israel Antiquities Authority sent more than a dozen teams of archaeologists on a top-secret operation just before the Israeli withdrawal, to scour that part of the area for ancient scrolls, "like Indiana Jones", wrote an Israeli journalist scornfully.

Contrary evidence can be smudged out, explained away, or simply ignored. A nationalist Israeli archaeologist was deplored by his colleagues for labelling obviously Christian sites as Jewish. Names disappear from maps along with the peoples who once lived there. When archaeological excavations called into question many of the key components of the Old Testament and its whole chronology, many fundamentalist Christians and Israelis refused to believe the findings or simply remained indifferent. Many ancient historians and archaeologists have come to believe that the Israelites may never have been in Egypt. If there was an exodus, it may have been only a small affair with a few families. The Israelites may not have conquered the land of the Canaanites, and Jericho probably did not have walls to fall down at the blast of a trumpet. The great kingdom of Solomon and David, which was said to stretch from the Mediterranean to the Euphrates, was more likely to have been a small chiefdom. Remains from the time indicate that Jerusalem was a small city, not the magnificent one of the Bible. So why, asked Ze'ev Herzog in the respected Israeli newspaper *Haaretz,* has what is a major change in views about the biblical past not provoked a reaction, even from secular Israelis? His conclusion is that they find it too painful to contemplate. "The blow to the mythical foundations of the Israeli identity is apparently too threatening, and it is more convenient to turn a blind eye."

Reactions have not always been so muted. Nadia Abu El-Haj, an American of Palestinian origin, came under ferocious attack for arguing that Israelis had used archaeology to reinforce their claims to Israel. "This is a book which should never have been published", commented a critic on the Amazon website. "This work is an effort to completely erase the historical connection of the Jewish people to the land of Israel." A vigorous campaign was undertaken to prevent her from getting tenure at Barnard College, where she was teaching. Historians who have examined Israeli history, as they would any other, trying to disentangle myth from fact and challenging accepted wisdom, have similarly found themselves in a minefield. The "new history" by historians such as Avi Shlaim and Benny Morris is, said Shabtai Teveth, a journalist and biographer of Israel's first prime minister, David Ben-Gurion, "a farrago of distortions, omissions, tendentious readings and outright falsifications". Israel, as we shall see, is by no means the only society to have its history wars, but because so much is at stake there, from the very identity of the nation to its right to exist on its land, the conflict can get ferocious.

7

HISTORY WARS

History is about remembering the past, but it is also about choosing to forget. In political campaigns, candidates challenge one another with what they have chosen not to put in their biographies. We do it in our personal lives. "You never told me that", we say angrily or with shock. "I never knew that about you". Some of the most difficult and protracted wars in societies around the world have been over what is being omitted or downplayed in the telling of their history – and what should be in. When people talk, as they frequently do, about the need for "proper" history, what they really mean is the history they want and like. School textbooks, university courses, movies, books, war memorials, art galleries and museums have all from time to time been caught up in debates that say as much about the present and its concerns as they do about the ostensible subject of history.

Educating the next generations and instilling in them the right views and values are things most societies take very seriously. The fact that so many countries, especially in the West, have received large immigrant populations has given the issue even more importance. Most Western societies have been shaken by evidence, acts of terrorism especially, that there are immigrants who are indifferent to the values of the host society and a smaller number who in fact actively despise them. Episodes like the murder of the controversial director Theo van Gogh or the discovery of a terrorist plot in Toronto have forced the Dutch and the Canadians to look at the ways in which they integrate, or fail to integrate, new arrivals. There are fears as well that even the well-established inhabitants do not properly understand their own societies or the key values they embody. As a result, there are repeated calls for the teaching of national values. (Finding agreement on what those might be is not always easy, as the case of France so clearly shows, where religious tolerance conflicts with a concern that Muslim immigrants become French and secular.)

History is often used as a series of moral tales, to enhance group solidarity or, more defensibly in my view, to explain how important institutions such as parliaments and concepts such as democracy developed, and so the teaching of the past has been central to the debates over how to instil and transmit values. The danger is that what may be an admirable goal can distort history either by making it into a simple narrative in which there are black-and-white characters or by depicting it as all tending in one direction, whether that of human progress or the triumph of a particular group. Such history flattens out the complexity of human experience and leaves no room for different interpretations of the past.

The motto of the province of Quebec is *"Je me souviens"*, and the French-speakers in particular do indeed remember, but often selectively. History, as taught in the Quebec schools, has stressed the continued existence of French-speakers as an embattled minority in an English Canada and how they have struggled unceasingly for their rights. When the Parti Québécois, the political expression of the separatist movement in Quebec, was in power in the 1990s, its education minister, Pauline Marois (now party leader), promised to double the time spent on history by high school students. Hard-line separatists were not satisfied: the curriculum, in their view, included too much world history and paid too much attention to English and aboriginal minorities in the province.

English-speaking Canadians have other fears, including that young Canadians are not learning enough about the past to give them pride in their country. The Dominion Institute conducts surveys every year and announces with much gloom that Canadians cannot identify their prime ministers or remember the dates when key events took place. In 1999, a group of philanthropists set up the Historica Foundation, whose mission is to fill in, as they see it, the gaps in the teaching of Canada's past. In Australia, John Howard, prime minister from 1996 to 2007, caused a spirited public debate when he announced that he had had enough of the "black armband" view of Australian history. The charge came at a difficult time, as Australians were considering what to do about the Stolen Generations of Aboriginal children who had been taken from their families and given to white families. Professional historians, Howard said, were "self-appointed cultural dieticians" who had persuaded Australians that their history is a sorry tale of racism, filled with crimes against the Aboriginals. Journalists and other commentators, appealing to the strong strain of anti-intellectualism in Australian culture, attacked the "moral mafia" and the "chattering classes" with glee. Most Australians, one columnist said, would be happy to see reconciliation between the Aboriginals and mainstream society, if only the former would "stop talking about the past".

In the United Kingdom, there are repeated debates over what history schoolchildren should be learning. Should it tell, as the Conservative Kenneth Baker wanted when he was minister of education, "how a free and democratic society had developed over the centuries"? Or should it be the history of those who were oppressed and marginalised? History from the top down or history from the bottom up? Do children need a chronology at all, or are they better off learning about topics such as the family or women or science and technology? In the summer of 2007, Ofsted, the body that inspects British schools, set off a national debate when it complained that the history being taught was too fragmented and that students had no idea when anything had taken place or in what order. Many parents had already discovered this for themselves and had made a surprise bestseller out of an Edwardian history for children. *Our Island Story* takes for granted that British history has moved onward and upward over the centuries, that the British Empire was a good thing, and that Britain was generally in the right. It is filled with stories, of Richard the Lion Heart, Sir Walter Raleigh, Robin Hood, and, of course, King Arthur. There are heroes and villains. A pre-Raphaelite Boadicea (as she was still known then) gallops across an illustrated page with her golden hair streaming behind her. A thoughtful Robert the Bruce watches a spider weaving its web and learns persistence. The two little princes tremble together as their evil uncle Richard III prepares to kill them. It is not good history – it has nothing to say about the new, multi-ethnic and multicultural Britain of today – but it is entertaining and may encourage children to take more of an interest in their country's past. The debates over what sort of history to teach often get entangled with the question, being hotly debated in so many countries today, of how to integrate immigrants into the host society. In the late 1980s and early 1990s, the Thatcher Conservatives worried that new arrivals were not being taught what it was to be British. Mrs Thatcher herself wanted a "patriotic history". More recently, the Labour Party's Gordon Brown, who would presumably disagree with her on the content of such history, said that those who want to become British citizens should be able to show that they understand British history and culture.

In the United States, it used to be taken for granted that immigrants would become assimilated into American society and that one of the most important ways of doing this was through the schools. The Civil War, perhaps because it showed how fragile the Union could be, stimulated a deep interest in American history. Textbooks showed a history that unfolded triumphantly from the early settlements and the Founding Fathers up to the present. Patriotic societies, by the hundreds, encouraged the veneration of the American flag and held parades and festivals to commemorate the great moments of the American past. Thanksgiving took on even greater importance as a time when Americans gathered to remember the founding of the nation. Theodore White, the distinguished journalist, remembered himself and his classmates, the children of Jewish immigrants from Central Europe, enacting the first meetings between the Pilgrim fathers and the local Indians. For him it was a part of becoming American. The newer Memorial Day, proclaimed after the Civil War, became a time to remember the dead soldiers. In many states, schools were required by law to teach American history and civics in a way that would encourage patriotism. Self-appointed guardians vetted textbooks to ensure that the right message was getting across. Arthur Schlesinger Sr., one of the giants of American history in the years between the two world wars, was roundly criticised by Irish Chicago politicians for writing a text that, in their view, promoted an unhealthy and unpatriotic admiration of the British and their institutions. In 1927, the mayor had a copy of one of his "treason-tainted" books publicly burned.

Because history has been so intertwined with Americans' views of themselves as a people and with making immigrants a part of that people, textbooks and curriculum in the schools have repeatedly stirred up public controversies. In 1990 the first President Bush unwittingly lit the fuse for the most recent explosion when he announced that the federal government would work with state governors to establish National Education Goals, partly to ensure that American students could compete in a world where education was increasingly important but also to prepare them to be good citizens. The Clinton administration, which succeeded in 1993, carried on with the project. One of the core subjects, along with English, mathematics, science and geography, where goals were to be set was history. After much debate and consultation, the National Council for History Standards produced a set of guidelines for American and world history which states could accept or not as they pleased. Although there was more stress on multiculturalism and on non-Western civilisations, those responsible for the guidelines felt confident that they were successfully telling the story of the United States in a way that would appeal to students. Moreover, they had included aspects of the past – women's or black history, for example – that had previously been neglected.

Shortly before the document was to be released, Lynne Cheney, wife of Dick Cheney, and a prominent conservative Republican herself, carried out what would have been called, in words familiar to the second Bush's administration, a preemptive attack. In an article in the *Wall Street Journal*, she deplored the proposed new standards, which, she argued, gave a "grim and gloomy" view of the American past. As she saw it, politically correct professors who were driven by a hatred of traditional political and chronological history had produced a story in which the Ku Klux Klan got more attention than Daniel Webster or Albert Einstein. Rush Limbaugh, the right-wing radio show host, was beside himself with patriotic righteousness. The historians responsible for the National History Standards, he said, were bent on inculcating in the young the belief that "our country is inherently evil". Others, including members of Congress, were not far behind. Those reformed criminals G. Gordon Liddy and Oliver North, now themselves hosting radio shows, talked about "the standards from hell". Senator Slade Gorton of Washington State denounced the standards in Congress as a vicious attack on Western civilisation. In the autumn of 1995, Senator Bob Dole, who was preparing his bid for the Republican presidential nomination, went even further. The standards, he said, were treasonous, "worse than external enemies".

The attacks did not go unanswered. Indeed, the United States found itself in a nationwide and far-reaching debate about what history was and what it should be for. Teachers and professional historians were delighted to see history restored to a central place in the curriculum. Liberals felt that the standards reflected the new, increasingly diverse United States. Many simply liked the stress on content and chronology. The *Los Angeles Times* said with approval, "Would that college graduates could all meet the standards for knowledge of the Constitution that are set here". In the end, after more discussion and revision, new guidelines were published in 1996. They included a new final section where students were asked to explore controversies over history itself.

The public and often bitter debate over the history standards was always about more than curriculum. It came at a time when the United States was uncertain about its role in the post-Cold War world and about its own society. The neoconservatives feared the United States no longer possessed the will to use its enormous power. At home, conservative Americans saw a decline in family values, which for them was often symbolised by legalised abortion. And many Americans worried about whether there truly was a central American identity anymore. Many of the new immigrants no longer appeared to want to be assimilated. Hispanics, for example, were insisting on keeping their own language and even having Spanish schools. Universities were abandoning their traditional Western civilisation courses, and American history courses increasingly focused on cultural and social history. If Americans did not share a common sense of the past, what would happen to the dream expressed in the widely used government motto *"E pluribus unum"*? Would it come to stand for "Out of the one, many," rather than the other way around? Although the particular furore over the National History Standards died down (indeed they have been widely adopted), the fear remains. In 2004, the respected historian Samuel Huntington published a melancholy book, *Who Are We?*, in which he warns that the "deconstructionist project" has elevated group and regional histories at the expense of national history. "People", he warns, "who are losing that memory are becoming something less than a nation".

In countries that are, for whatever reason, lacking in self-confidence, the teaching of history can be an even more sensitive matter. In Turkey the government takes a strong interest in the curriculum. Historians who argue for greater attention being paid to the history of Turkey's minorities or who dare to suggest that there was an Armenian genocide in World War I can find themselves in serious trouble. In Russia, President Vladimir Putin took a personal interest in the writing of new "patriotic" history textbooks being used in the schools. He handed out grants to approved authors (one was a former professor of Marxist-Leninist social science who had transformed himself into a historian), and his government gave itself the powers to determine what textbooks were used. At a teachers' conference at the Kremlin in June 2007, Putin praised the new textbooks. "Many school books are written by people who work to get foreign grants", he said. "They dance to the polka that others have paid for. You understand?" Just in case the assembled teachers missed his point, he told them that the time had come to get rid of the "muddle" and have a more openly nationalistic view of the past. The new textbooks, he said, would present a proper view of Stalin and of his place in Russian history. There were, Putin admitted to the teachers, some "problematic pages" in Russia's past but far fewer than in other countries. (And look how the United States had behaved in Vietnam.) Stalin was a dictator, but that was necessary at the time to save Russia from its enemies. In the great struggle of the Cold War, which, according to the manual, was started by the United States, "democratisation was not an option".

In China, the Party's propaganda and education departments keep a close eye on the schools to ensure that they teach students of the suffering of the Chinese at the hands of the imperialists and convey the lesson that history selected the Communist Party to lead China into its present happy state. (In imperial China, the mandate was conferred by heaven, but the idea is much the same.) Recently, the authorities closed down a journal called *Freezing Point* after it carried an essay by Yuan Weishi, a well-known Chinese historian, in which he pointed out that high-school textbooks were filled with errors and distortions. What is more, they gave highly slanted views of the Chinese past, to show, he argued, that Chinese civilisation is superior to all others and that foreign culture should be seen as a threat. What really got him and the journal into trouble was the assertion that history, as it was being taught, justified the use of political power and even violence to keep people on the right path. Professor Yuan's views, the authorities said, were heretical and attacked "socialism and the leadership by the party".

In Shanghai, a group of academics boldly produced new

school textbooks which gave less space to the old staples of Chinese Communist history such as the depredations of imperialism and the rise of the Chinese Communist Party and paid more attention to other cultures and to such topics as technology and economics. The texts also let it be known that there could be more than one viewpoint on the past. Their fatal mistake, however, was to downplay the role of Mao. When a *New York Times* article headed "Where's Mao?" commented on the improvement over the old two-dimensional histories, the authorities swung into action. Historians in Beijing issued a statement: "The Shanghai textbooks depart from Marxist historical materialism, and simply narrate events, rather than explain their nature. There are serious mistakes in political direction, theoretical direction, and academic direction." The texts were banned.

Fortunately, the teaching of history can change for the better. In South Africa, since the end of apartheid, the schools, as part of the national project of truth and reconciliation, have tried to present a history that includes all South Africans. In the Republic of Ireland, history used to be similarly circumscribed by political pressure. The story told in the schools was a simple one: eight centuries of oppression and then the triumph of Irish nationalism in the 1920s. Episodes that did not fit this version – the civil war, for example, between the competing nationalists – were ignored. Today, as its president pointed out, the schools teach a much fuller and more rounded version – and let the students know that there may be more than one way of viewing the past.

Schools are only one battleground. In Australia, John Howard and the more conservative media also went after the new National Museum on the grounds that it presented the past as white Australia's genocide against the Aboriginals and failed to highlight the great explorers and entrepreneurs who built up the country. Museums, especially ones that involve history, occupy a curious place in our minds. Is their purpose to commemorate or to teach? To answer questions or to raise them? The answer in most societies is not clear. The Chinese, for example, have what are described as museums of World War II but more resemble Madame Tussauds waxworks than the Royal Ontario Museum or the British Museum. Instead of labelled objects in glass cases, they feature tableaux where Japanese soldiers bayonet Chinese civilians and Japanese doctors bend over the victims of their hideous experiments. The distinction between museums and memorials is a blurred one and, as a result, gives rise to often angry debates over how the past should be portrayed and interpreted.

In 1994, as the war over the National History Standards was heating up, the Smithsonian Institution in Washington started to plan an exhibit to commemorate the end of World War II. One of its holdings was the B-29 bomber which had dropped the atomic bomb on Hiroshima. The *Enola Gay*, named by its pilot after his mother, became the centre of a huge controversy when the curators suggested that visitors might want to think about the morality of using the world's newest and most destructive weapon. Part of the exhibit was to be broken objects retrieved from the rubble at Hiroshima and Nagasaki. Although the museum had consulted with special interest groups, including veterans' associations, and with historians, this did not spare it the storm that followed.

The Smithsonian curators tried, naively perhaps, to use the *Enola Gay* to raise questions about the nature of modern war and the role of nuclear weapons. They also hoped to inform the public that the decision to drop the atomic bombs on Hiroshima and then Nagasaki had been controversial at the time and had remained so. Such explorations of issues ran up against those who felt strongly that the National Air and Space Museum existed not to encourage public debate, but to commemorate the glories of flight and of airpower and to reinforce Americans' patriotism. Neoconservatives charged that the Smithsonian and liberal historians were attacking the record of the United States in World War II and American society itself by suggesting that Hiroshima had been of questionable morality. *The Washington Times* found something sinister in the fact that the lead curator was both a Canadian and a former professor. Veterans resented the implication that their war had not been entirely a good one. The first script for the exhibit contained two sentences, subsequently deleted, which were quoted repeatedly as examples of the Smithsonian's reprehensible rewriting of history. For most Americans, the early version said, the war against Japan "was fundamentally different than the one waged against Germany and Italy – it was a war of vengeance". (It was ironic that some of the Smithsonian's critics said the exhibit should include as part of the context Japanese atrocities such as the rape of Nanjing and the Bataan death march.) Even worse, from the point of view of the veterans and their supporters, the text then went on to say that for most Japanese, "it was a war to defend their unique culture against Western imperialism". The American Air Force Association charged that the exhibit claimed there was moral equivalency between the United States and Japan. Almost worse, perhaps, from the association's viewpoint, it was a "strident attack" on the value of airpower.

Members of Congress, newspapers and right-wing radio talk shows jumped in enthusiastically to charge that the Smithsonian was besmirching the honour of the United States and its war heroes. George Will said the Smithsonian and the National History Standards were equally infected with the "cranky anti-Americanism of the campuses". Pat Buchanan, who was soon to announce his candidacy for the 1996 Republican presidential nomination, saw the exhibit as part of "a sleepless campaign to inculcate in American youth a revulsion toward America's past". Nancy Kassebaum, a Republican senator from Kansas, introduced a resolution in the Senate which declared that the exhibit's script was offensive and directed the National Air and Space Museum not to impugn "the memory of those who gave their lives for freedom". In an election year, no one was going to vote against such sentiments. The Smithsonian had retreated step by step, redoing the script and the exhibits repeatedly, but the attacks merely increased. In January 1995 it cancelled the show. Four months later, the director of the National Air and Space Museum resigned.

Canada has just gone through a similar dispute, and yet again it is over the way a museum chose to commemorate World War II. When the new War Museum opened in Ottawa in 2005, it was widely hailed as a stunning building with detailed and well-planned exhibits showing Canada at war from its earliest days to its twenty-first-century campaign in Afghanistan. Nevertheless, the museum almost immediately ran into trouble over the part of its exhibit devoted to the bombing campaign against Germany between 1939 and 1945. As I mentioned earlier, the plaque titled "An Enduring Controversy" gave particular offence to veterans and their supporters. It called attention to the continuing debate over both the efficacy and the morality of the strategy of the Royal Air Force's Bomber Command (and its head, Sir Arthur "Bomber" Harris), which sought to destroy Germany's capacity to fight on by massive bombing of German industrial and civilian targets. The veterans were also upset by photographs that showed dead Germans lying amid shattered buildings after bombing attacks.

The issue was almost bound to cause trouble with the veterans because so many Canadians – about twenty thousand – had flown with the RAF's Bomber Command and nearly ten thousand had died. Furthermore, the veterans had already fought a similar battle a decade previously when they had taken on the Canadian Broadcasting Corporation over a television series it ran in 1992 on Canadian participation in World War II. One segment of *The Valour and the Horror* suggested that Canadian airmen, brave as they were, had been led into carrying out a morally dubious bombing campaign by their unscrupulous leaders. The veterans organised petitions and letter-writing campaigns against the series and the CBC. Conservative members of Parliament asked hostile questions in the House of Commons, and the hitherto-obscure Senate Subcommittee on Veterans Affairs started a portentous series of hearings. By the summer of 1993, a group of air force veterans was suing the makers of the documentaries for a huge amount in damages. It was, said the lawyer for the veterans, quite simply "about right and wrong; good and evil; white and black; truth and falsehood". The suit made its way to the Supreme Court, which finally ruled it out of order. The CBC made a commitment to the veterans not to rebroadcast the series.

Since the veterans and their supporters had won that battle to their satisfaction, they were more than ready to take on the bombing exhibit. *Legion Magazine*, in an article titled "At War with the Museum", said, "The war museum has proceeded in such an insensitive and hurtful way that many air veterans feel they and their fallen comrades are being fingered as immoral – even criminal – by an institution of the very government that sent them on those harrowing missions". The letters started to come in, accusing the museum of labelling Canadian pilots as war criminals. Yet again, those who took part in history were said to have a better view of what had happened than those who studied it later. Official Ottawa, which has tended to have an exaggerated sense of the veterans' power, was more than ready to try to find a compromise before things got out of hand again. Hoping to defuse the criticisms, the museum's director called in four outside historians (of which I was one) to give their opinions on the exhibit. Unfortunately, they split. Two tried to uphold the standards of their profession by saying that, yes, there was indeed a controversy over the bombing but that the presentation was "unbalanced." And was it really necessary, asked one, to refer visitors to a controversy that was quite a complicated one, best carried on among experts? "If we even need to ask the question", he concluded, "then the answer is no". The other two historians took the view that museums must be places of learning, and that when there are controversies, they ought to say so. "History", I concluded, "should not be written to make the present generation feel good but to remind us that human affairs are complicated".

The Senate Subcommittee on Veterans Affairs roused itself from its customary torpor and held a series of hearings in the spring of 2007 in which the veterans featured prominently. Its report recommended to the War Museum that it take steps to sort out the dispute with the veterans. The museum, it said, ought to "consider alternative ways of presenting an equally historically accurate version of its material, in a manner which eliminates the sense of insult felt by aircrew veterans and removes potential for further misinterpretation by the public". What that meant soon became apparent. The War Museum's director left in circumstances that are still not clear, and soon after, the museum announced that it was going to work on revised wording for the exhibit in consultation with the veterans. Cliff Chadderton, chairman of the National Council of Veteran Associations in Canada, was ungracious in victory. "We don't know what took them so long, because it's patently wrong, the text of the panel." He promised more trouble if he and his veterans did not like the revised wording.

Like many other countries, Canada has also had its disputes

over public holidays. Many objected when Dominion Day, a celebration which dated back to the formation of Canada as a self-governing dominion within the British Empire, was renamed Canada Day in 1982. Others argued that since Canada had just cut its last legal tie to the United Kingdom, the new name was a mark of full nationhood. In the United States, Columbus Day has caused even greater trouble in recent years. Originally intended to celebrate the discovery (itself now a contentious term) of the New World (another source of contention) by Christopher Columbus in October 1492, it now pits Native Americans – who argue that Columbus's arrival was a very bad thing for them and Columbus himself a murderous thug – against Italian Americans who take the opposite view. Hugo Chávez of Venezuela, who was never slow to jump on a bandwagon if he knew it was going to gain him publicity and simultaneously annoy the United States, has renamed the holiday in his country as Indigenous Resistance Day. The five hundredth anniversary of Columbus's landing in the Caribbean was particularly tricky. In the lead-up to 1992, three hundred indigenous Americans met in Quito to talk about five hundred years of resistance. In the United States, the protestant National Council of Churches attempted to make amends by weighing in with talk of invasion, genocide, slavery, "ecocide" and exploitation of the land as Columbus's true legacy. The Reagan administration, not relishing this particular battle against the forces of political correctness, hastily renamed the official commemoration a jubilee and not a celebration. That did not stop conservatives from accusing liberals in the universities and elsewhere of hating the United States so much that they wanted to deny its European roots.

The more complicated the past, the more difficult the commemoration. West Germany, as it then was, could not decide how to celebrate the two hundredth anniversary of the death of

Frederick the Great. Were they remembering the scholar or the soldier? Was he a figure of the Enlightenment or a forerunner of Hitler? Almost everyone in France agreed that 1989, the two-hundredth anniversary of the French Revolution, ought to be commemorated. But what did the Revolution mean? Was it to be celebrated for liberty, equality, fraternity, or deplored for the Terror? The members of the commission supposedly responsible for the commemorations quarrelled among themselves and with the government. In the end, the national celebrations were taken in hand by an impresario who staged a marvellous and eccentric parade – the Festival of the Planet's Tribes – through Paris. With the funky chicken, African drums, Russian soldiers marching in fake snow, Chinese students towing a huge drum, and a marching band from Florida, should the new slogan for France be, *Newsweek* wondered, "Liberty, Frivolity, Irony"?

If the significance of the French Revolution is difficult for the French to agree on, so, too, is much else in France's history. What about Napoleon? Is he a great national hero or, as a French historian recently charged, a racist dictator? Should the major anniversaries such as his great victory at Austerlitz be commemorated as the British commemorated the bicentennial of the Battle of Trafalgar, or should they be passed over in silence? How should French schools present the history of French colonialism in Algeria? For many years, the savage war between the Algerian nationalists on the one hand and the French settlers and the French army on the other was officially downplayed as "the events". The pervasive and sanctioned use of torture against the Algerians became a matter of public discussion only when General Paul Aussaresses, who was a high-ranking intelligence officer during the Algerian war, publicly defended the use of torture in 2000. (After September 11, he recommended using his methods on Al Qaeda.) In 2005, the government passed a law stipulating that textbooks should recognise "the positive role of the French presence in its overseas colonies, especially in North Africa". At first a few historians protested against this attempt at an official history, but when the nation was shaken that autumn by rioting adolescents of North African descent, the issue hit the headlines and the National Assembly.

The right-wing, collaborationist Vichy regime, which ruled over what was left of France by the Germans during World War II, has been particularly difficult for the French to deal with. For a long time after 1945, they told themselves a comforting story that ignored the degree of support Vichy had among the population as well as its often enthusiastic collaboration with the Nazis. When he arrived in triumph in Paris in 1944, General Charles de Gaulle, the leader of the Free French, announced that Vichy was "a non-event and without consequence". The true France was represented by his own forces and the Resistance. The few French who had collaborated were to be punished, and the French would get on with rebuilding their great country. The myth, for that is what it was, allowed the French to forget about the French policemen who willingly rounded up the Jews to be deported to the death camps; to forget the relatively small number who joined the Resistance and the many officials of the old regime who had collaborated and yet were allowed to continue in their positions after 1945. The government made little attempt to catch and try some of France's more prominent war criminals such as Klaus Barbie, the "Butcher of Lyon". Indeed, some received protection from the Church or from highly placed politicians. No one questioned, or not until the 1990s, the claim of François Mitterrand, president from 1981 to 1995, that he had worked for the Vichy government for only a short period before joining the Resistance. In fact, as an enterprising journalist discovered, he had worked there for much longer than he had admitted and had won a decoration.

The process by which France has come to terms with its Vichy past has been a painful one. Initially, it was only foreign historians who chose to examine the period carefully. When the filmmaker Marcel Ophüls made his classic documentary *The Sorrow and the Pity*, which gave a truer picture of Vichy and shattered the myth of widespread resistance, French television refused to broadcast it. When it was released in 1971, it was attacked from the Right and the Left. Jean-Paul Sartre found it "inaccurate". A conservative commentator in *Le Monde* scolded the Jews who had been interviewed in the film for their ingratitude in criticising Vichy's president, Marshal Pétain, who, he claimed, had saved them. In the 1970s and 1980s, there was increasing public discussion, with more films and books appearing, but it was not until the end of the century, after Mitterrand and much of his generation had passed from the scene, that the new French president, Jacques Chirac, was able to admit that France had aided in the Holocaust.

In Russia, where the transition from one form of government to another was much more abrupt, post-Soviet governments have been grappling, with limited success, to make a new identity for Russia by using history. "These days", the Russians say, "we live in a country with an unpredictable past". While the new order clearly does not want to celebrate the November 7 anniversary of the Bolshevik Revolution of 1917, it does not want to alienate the citizenry by getting rid of what has been a two-day holiday. When Boris Yeltsin was in power, he kept the holiday but renamed it the Day of Accord and Reconciliation. The public remained largely in ignorance of the change. In 2005, Putin moved the holiday a couple of days forward, to November 4, and christened it the Day of National Unity. The change in date is to commemorate Russian success in driving out Polish invaders in 1612. The public, apart from the radical nationalists, still has no idea of what the holiday is supposed to be celebrating.

What present-day Russia has shown little interest in remembering, at least so far, is the horrors of the Stalinist period. There are few official museums or sites to mark the Gulag or the thousands upon thousands who died in Stalin's prisons, and few memorials to those brave individuals, like Andrei Sakharov, who opposed the Soviet state.

Russia is not alone in wanting to turn its eyes firmly away from the painful parts of the past. In the decade after the Vietnam War ended, the United States, unlike the case in all previous wars, did not undertake to create an official war memorial to the dead. It was only when private citizens created their own foundation that the government was shamed into providing a piece of land on the Mall in Washington.

In Spain, when democracy gradually took root after General Franco's death in 1975, there was an unspoken agreement – the *"pacto del olvido"* – to forget the trauma of the civil war and the years of repression that followed. In recent decades, though, writers, historians and filmmakers began to explore the horrors of the war, and in November 2007 the government enacted the Law of Historical Memory. There is to be a national effort to locate the mass graves and identify the bones of those who were shot by Franco's winning side. Franco's regime itself has been formally repudiated, and it will be erased, as much as possible, from public commemoration. Franco's statues will disappear, and the names of streets and squares will be changed. It is unlikely that the law will bring agreement on Spain's history. If anything, it is opening up old divisions and creating new ones. "What do we gain?" asks Manuel Fraga, a senator and former minister under Franco who took part in the transition to democracy. "Look at the British: Cromwell decapitated a king, but his statue still stands outside parliament. You cannot change the past".

West Germany and Japan were both pushed to remember the

recent past by the victors in World War II but also, to be fair, by their own citizens. Immediately after the war, the Germans, like other Europeans, were preoccupied with survival and rebuilding and had little inclination or energy to spend on thinking about the past. Perhaps, too, because their defeat had been so complete and the Nazi past was so hideous (and their own complicity with Hitler so profound), they took refuge in forgetting and in silence. In the 1950s, few ordinary Germans wanted to discuss Nazism or remind one another of their involvement with the regime. With the one exception of Anne Frank's *Diary of a Young Girl*, which sold very well, the dozens of memoirs by concentration camp survivors and the few essays on German guilt did not attract much attention. The silence about the past was never complete, though; there were always writers and thinkers prepared to ask the awkward questions, and Germans could not entirely escape the consequences of following Hitler when their country was first occupied and then divided into two independent states. Moreover, West Germany, on Chancellor Konrad Adenauer's initiative, paid reparations to Israel. (Only 11 per cent of Germans at the time thought the decision was a good one.)

It was at the end of the 1950s that West Germans started to examine their own past in depth. In 1961, the trial of Adolf Eichmann in Jerusalem exposed the elaborate bureaucracy with which the Nazi state had carried out the extermination of the Jews. Other trials followed in West Germany, and a younger, more radical generation began to demand and get the truth about the past. When the American television series *Holocaust* was shown on German television in 1979, over half the adult population watched it. Today, a reunited Germany stands out as a society that deals with its past, often in very visible ways. More concentration camp museums have been opened, and school-children are taken to see them as a matter of course. In Berlin, the National Memorial for the Victims of War and Tyranny, the bombed-out ruins of the Kaiser Wilhelm Memorial Church, and the Holocaust memorial all act as a national remembrance, while all over Germany towns and cities have their own memorials and museums.

During the Cold War, while West Germans were confronting their Nazi past, East Germans were avoiding it. The Communist state of East Germany managed to detach itself from all connection to or responsibility for the Nazi period. Hitler and the Nazis were said to represent the final stage of capitalism. It was they who had started the war and they who had killed millions of Jews and other Europeans. East Germany was socialist and progressive and had always stood side by side with the Soviet Union against Fascism. Indeed, a significant number of East Germans grew up thinking their country had fought on the Soviet side in World War II. Although the East German regime made memorials of three of the concentration camps, the only deaths remembered were those of Communists; Jews and Gypsies were not mentioned.

Austria's amnesia was even more striking. In the decades after World War II, it managed, very successfully, to portray itself as the first victim of Nazism. In a 1945 ceremony in Vienna for a memorial to fallen Soviet soldiers, Leopold Figl, who was shortly to become the country's chancellor, mourned that "the people of Austria have spent seven years languishing under Hitler's barbarity". Austrians comforted themselves for the next decades with such assurances. They were a happy, gentle people who had never wanted to be joined with the likes of Nazi Germany; Hitler had forced the *Anschluss* on them. They had never wanted war, and if their soldiers had fought, it was only to defend their homeland. And they had suffered hugely, it must be said, at the hands of the Allies. Who, after all, had destroyed the magnificent opera house in Vienna? The fact that many of the most fervent Nazis, including Hitler himself, were Austrian; the wildly enthusiastic crowds that greeted his triumphal march to Vienna in 1938; and the willing collaboration of many Austrians in the persecution and destruction of the Jews – all that was simply brushed under the carpet. The few brave liberals who tried to both celebrate the small Austrian resistance to Nazism and memorialise the destruction of the Jews found themselves isolated and accused of being Communists. It was only in the 1960s, with new generations appearing on the scene and Germany's own examination of its Nazi past, that questions about Austria's role began to surface.

The Japanese are often compared unfavorably to the West Germans, especially by the Chinese. Japan has not, it is charged, admitted its culpability in the invasion of China in the 1930s, its role in the start of the Pacific war, and the savage treatment of those it conquered, from the rape of Nanjing to its inhumane medical experiments in Manchuria. There is enough truth in this to make the accusations stick. Japan, like Austria, portrayed itself as a victim in the years after the war. It used the bombing of Hiroshima and Nagasaki in part as a way of deflecting attention from its own crimes. It was slow to offer compensation, for example, to the Korean women it forced to serve as prostitutes for its soldiers. Successive prime ministers have paid their respects to the Yasukuni Shrine, which honours Japan's war dead, including leaders who were convicted of war crimes.

On the other hand, there has been a long-lasting public debate over how to deal with the difficult parts of the past. Even in the 1950s, a trickle of books and articles came out, many of them by eyewitnesses and participants, which confirmed that Japanese soldiers had indeed committed atrocities. Meanwhile, a handful of historians wrote texts in which they insisted on dealing with all aspects of the war. While the nationalists have attacked such writings, they have not been able to prevent them from appearing. Nor is it true, as the Chinese like to claim, that Japanese students have been kept ignorant of what went on in the war. (The attack also comes strangely from a country where whole pieces of the past, such as the Cultural Revolution, cannot be examined at all.) By the 1970s, for example, Japanese school texts were mentioning the Nanjing massacre and giving figures for those who were killed. For many Japanese, that decade marked a moment when their nation moved from being a victim to being a victimiser. In the 1980s, when nationalists tried to downplay Japanese aggression and the wartime atrocities, their attempt set off a furious reaction from liberals and a full-scale public debate. Scholars began to broaden their research into lesser-known episodes and aspects of the war. In December 1997, on the anniversary of the Nanjing massacre, a citizens' parade, which included visiting Chinese and German scholars, walked through Tokyo behind a special lantern bearing the Chinese characters for "to commemorate".

History has so often produced conflicts, but it can also help in bringing about reconciliation. The purpose of the truth and reconciliation commissions in South Africa and Chile was to expose the past in all its seaminess and to move on. That does not mean dwelling on past sufferings or past misdeeds to the exclusion of all else, but accepting that they have occurred and trying to assess their meaning. When John Howard was trying to promote a national history curriculum in Australia, the principal of a girls' high school in Sydney described how she dealt with the contested story of the arrival of the first whites. "We canvass all the terms for white settlement: colonialism, invasion and genocide." Examining the past honestly, whether that is painful for some people or not, is the only way for societies to become mature and to build bridges to others.

In 2006, those old enemies France and Germany brought out a joint history textbook, which students in both countries will use. Although it only deals with the period after World War II, the longer-term plan is to produce texts dealing with the more difficult subject of the period before 1945. In the Middle East, Sami Adwan, a Palestinian professor at Bethlehem University, has been working with an Israeli psychologist, Dan Bar-On, to design a text that both Israeli and Palestinian high school students can use. Their goals are more modest than the French and German ones; they hope merely to include the two different national histories side by side, as well as instances of cooperation and peace between Israelis and Palestinians to offset the prevailing stories of perpetual conflict. This, they hope, will help build a mutual understanding that will have a wider significance in the longer run. "In order for Palestinian and Israeli children to understand themselves", Professor Adwan told an interviewer, "they must understand the other. It is only after they understand the story of the other that they will discover to what extent they are truly prepared to understand the other side, and thus prepared to make changes to their own stories". So far, sadly, only a handful of teachers on both sides of the divide have shown an interest in using the text.

Public acts where the past is admitted can also help to heal wounds between countries. Chancellor Willy Brandt, on the first visit of a West German leader to Poland, made a huge impact when he fell to his knees before the memorial to the Warsaw Ghetto. In 1984, Mitterrand and Helmut Kohl, the German chancellor, met at Verdun, site of the most prolonged and deadly battle between their two countries in World War I, to celebrate the future of an integrated Europe. The two countries have also built a shared war museum at Péronne, which was once the German headquarters for the Battle of the Somme. The museum was designed to show the war as a European phenomenon and to stress the need for integration in present-day Europe.

Sometimes, of course, like a strong medicine, admitting past crimes can kill. The Soviet Union did not survive Mikhail Gorbachev's policy of glasnost, of opening up discussion of the Stalinist past. The revelations of the extent of the Gulag and the number of Stalin's victims served to undermine public faith in the whole system that could have produced such crimes. And the Soviet Union's admission in the 1980s, after years of denial, that it had indeed agreed secretly with Hitler to divide up the countries that lay between them and that its armies had murdered Polish soldiers after they had surrendered in 1939 only destroyed still further the hold that the Soviets had over Eastern Europe. (Today, the Russian media are backing away from that admission and returning to the old, false charge that the murders were done by the Nazis.) Then, one can ask, should such a regime and such an empire have survived?

8

HISTORY AS A GUIDE

History, as we have seen, is much used, but is it much use? On that, opinion has been divided ever since the fifth century B.C. when Thucydides declared the past was an aid in the interpretation of the future. Edward Gibbon regarded it rather as "the register of the crimes, follies and misfortunes of mankind". A. J. P. Taylor, contrarian in this as in so much else, believed that history was an enjoyable exercise which had no use whatsoever beyond helping us to understand the past. "Of course", he said dismissively, "you can learn certain commonplaces, such as that all men die or that one day, the deterrent, whatever it may be, will fail to deter". Perhaps it is best to ask if we would be worse off in the present if we did not know any history at all. I think the answer would probably be yes.

To begin with, history helps us to understand: first, those with whom we have to deal, and, second, and this is equally important, ourselves. As the American historian John Lewis Gaddis put it, it is like looking in a rearview mirror: if you only look back, you will land in the ditch, but it helps to know where you have come from and who else is on the road. One of the factors that made the Cold War so dangerous to both sides is that they simply did not understand each other. The Americans took the Soviets' rhetoric at face value and took for granted that their leadership really was out for world domination. The Communists, whether Soviet or Chinese, assumed that capitalist countries such as the United States and Britain would inevitably come to blows in their increasingly ruthless struggle for profits.

Michael Howard, the British military historian, despaired of the attitude that prevailed in Washington for much of the Cold War. "The Soviet Union was seen in the USA as a force of cosmic evil whose policy and intentions could be divined simply by multiplying Marxist dogma by Soviet military capacity." Many of the Soviet goals were, in fact, traditional Russian ones, dictated by geography and history. Russia has few natural borders and has suffered repeated invasions; its governments have always sought buffer zones to protect the Russian heartland. When Stalin took the opportunity to move into Eastern Europe at the end of World War II, he was motivated as much by a desire for security as by ideology and national pride, Russian national pride, for all that he came from Georgia. During the war he created new military honours named after not Marx or Lenin but great czarist generals and admirals. One evening at the end of the war, after a dinner with his intimates, Stalin spread a map out on a table and happily pointed to all the old czarist territory he had regained.

American strategists also assumed that the Kremlin was prepared to risk all-out war in pursuit of its goals. In fact, given the Soviet Union's huge losses in both world wars and the enormous job of reconstruction that lay before it after 1945, it was equally likely that the Soviet leadership would do a great deal to avoid war. We now know that was, in fact, often the case. When Nikita Khrushchev put nuclear-tipped missiles into Cuba in 1962, part of his motive was to let the United States feel what it was like to fear direct attack and the devastation of its land, something the Soviets knew so well. And when he pulled them out, it was because he did not want to live through another, even more deadly war than the two he had already survived.

In 1949, when the Communists won in China, the Americans knew far more about China than they did about the Soviet Union, but they still got it wrong. The pessimists who believed that the Chinese Communists really were placing themselves under Stalin's orders drowned out those few experts on China who suggested that with such different histories and cultures, it was probably only a matter of time before the two Communist powers fell out. Mao, they predicted, would be the Asian Tito. (The Yugoslav Communist leader had just fallen out very dramatically with Stalin.) And indeed, that is exactly what happened a decade later. When the Sino-Soviet split occurred, some hard-liners in the West could not bring themselves to believe it, arguing that the public recriminations between Beijing and Moscow were evidence of the extraordinary duplicity and deviousness of Communists.

The Communists usually misread the West just as badly, even though they had a much easier time in getting information. The Soviets expected Western powers to try to destroy them because, after all, wasn't that what they had done when they sent troops to intervene in the Russian civil war? In fact, Western intervention, even though it was supported noisily by people like Winston Churchill, was half-hearted; at the end of World War I, there was little stomach for further military adventures in countries such as Britain and France. The Marxist blinkers were powerful ones, and what they learned about the West and its history only reinforced their preconceptions. Even young Soviet diplomats in training were only allowed to read the Communist newspapers from Western countries. Capitalism would continue to grind the workers down, as it always had, and there would eventually be revolutions in countries such as the United Kingdom and the United States. Talk of democracy, public opinion, or the rule of law in such places was just that – talk. When American presidents, Jimmy Carter and Bill Clinton among them, raised issues of human rights, Communist leaders saw it as merely a way of interfering in their internal affairs.

If you do not know the history of another people, you will not understand their values, their fears and their hopes or how they are likely to react to something you do. There is another way of getting things wrong and that is to assume that other peoples are just like you. Robert McNamara has spent much of his life trying to come to terms with what went wrong with the American war in Vietnam. In his memoir, *In Retrospect,* he came up with lessons he hoped future leaders might heed. "We viewed", he says in one, "the people and leaders of South Vietnam in terms of our own experience. We saw in them a thirst for – and a determination to fight for – freedom and democracy". The United States failed equally to understand the determination of the North Vietnamese. Time and again, it assumed that it could raise the pain it was inflicting on the North to the point where its leaders would do a cost-benefit analysis and decide that the time had come to throw in the towel. Yet these were the people who had fought for seven years to defeat the French. "Our misjudgments of friend and foe alike", McNamara concluded sadly, "reflected our profound ignorance of the history, culture and politics of the people in the area and the personalities and habits of their leaders".

It was not a lesson the Bush White House of recent years appears to have learned. You believe in studying reality, a senior adviser said contemptuously to the journalist Ron Suskind in 2002. "That's not the way the world really works anymore", he continued. "We're an empire now, and when we act, we create our own reality. And while you're studying that reality – judiciously, as you will – we'll act again, creating other new realities, which you can study too, and that's how things will sort out. We're history's actors ... and you, all of you, will be left to just study what we do." If the White House had studied reality a bit more, the president might not have used the word "crusade" two days after September 11 to refer to how he intended to deal with terrorists. Muslims, even moderate ones, tend to react viscerally to being reminded of much earlier attacks from the West. If some attention had been paid to reality, the United States and the United Kingdom might not have been quite so surprised that Iraqis failed to welcome them or appreciate foreign control of their oil.

In November 2002, four months before the invasion of Iraq, Tony Blair had his only meeting with independent British experts. "We all pretty much said the same thing", said George Joffe, a Middle East specialist from Cambridge University. "Iraq is a very complicated country, there are tremendous intercommunal resentments, and don't imagine you'll be welcomed." Blair did not appear interested in this analysis and focused instead on Saddam Hussein: "But the man's uniquely evil, isn't he?" The experts tried to explain that thirty years of Hussein's dictatorship had ground down Iraq's civil society to the point that there were virtually no independent organised forces to serve as allies for the coalition. Blair remained uninterested. The Foreign Office showed no more interest in taking advantage of their considerable knowledge and expertise.

A little more than five years later, in January 2008, the U.K. Ministry of Defence issued a report that was severely critical of the way in which British soldiers were prepared to serve in Iraq. There had been, the report said, a lack of information about the context the soldiers would be operating in and uncertainty about how the Iraqis might react to an invasion. The military, the report went on, failed to anticipate differences between Iraq and the Balkans and Northern Ireland, where British forces had gained a great deal of their recent experience. In other words, they had not looked at the history of Iraq.

Knowing history can help avoid lazy generalisations as well. It would be folly to take on the Serbs, said the pessimists as Yugoslavia was falling to pieces; look how they fought off the Nazis in World War II. In fact, if you look more closely at what happened, as an American army researcher did a few years ago, you find that the German divisions were not the cream of the German army and most were seriously understrength. And if you look even further back, at World War I, you see that the Serbian army was defeated and forced into exile, and Serbia itself was occupied until the end of the war by German and Austrian troops. Afghanistan comes in for much the same rhetoric of despair; it has never, the pundits say, been conquered by an outside power. That would come as a surprise to Alexander the Great as much as to Genghis Khan. Today, we hear that the Western powers cannot interfere in the increasing chaos and misery of Zimbabwe because it would only rouse memories of colonialism among the population. It is a pity that such considerations were not taken into account when the United States went into Vietnam or, more recently, into Iraq.

History can also help in self-knowledge. The favourable light we so often see ourselves in can cast shadows as well. Canadians, for example, see themselves as a benevolent force in the world; they tend to overlook the fact that among rich countries, ours has provided a surprisingly small amount of foreign aid in past decades. Although Canadians pride themselves on being peace-keepers, they often do not know that Canada fought in four major wars in the twentieth century, from the South African one to the Korean. Americans tend to think of themselves as a peace-loving people who have never willingly picked a fight. "Our country has never started a war", President Ronald Reagan said in 1983. "Our sole objective is deterrence, the strength and capability it takes to prevent war". That is not how it might seem to the Mexicans or the Nicaraguans or the Cubans or, today, the Iraqis.

George Santayana's famous "Those who cannot remember the past are condemned to repeat it" is one of those overused dicta politicians and others offer up when they want to sound profound. It is true, however, that history reminds us usefully about the sorts of situations that have caused trouble in the past. Allied leaders in World War II were determined that this time, Germany and the other Axis powers would not be able to claim that they had never been defeated on the battlefield. Allied policy was one of unconditional surrender, and Germany, Japan and Italy were all occupied at the end of the war, and serious attempts, not all of them successful, were made to remodel their societies so that they would no longer be undemocratic and militaristic. When someone complained that such treatment was like the savage peace the Romans imposed on Carthage, the American general Mark Clark noted that no one heard much of the Carthaginians these days.

When President Franklin Delano Roosevelt and other Western leaders were starting to plan for the postwar world, they had the recent past very much in their minds in other ways. They wanted to build a robust world order which would prevent the world from sliding, yet again, into a deadly conflict. The interwar years had been unstable ones, partly because the League of Nations had not been strong enough. Key powers, the United States in particular, had not joined or, like Germany and Japan, had dropped out. This time, Roosevelt was determined, the United States should be a member of the new United Nations. He was also prepared to do a good deal to keep the Soviet Union in and the world stable and prosperous. What had been a precariously balanced international order of the 1920s had been put under further strain in the 1930s by the Great Depression, which encouraged countries to turn inward, throwing up tariff walls to protect their own workers and their own industries. What may have made sense for individual nations was disastrous for the world as a whole. Trade and investment dropped off sharply, and national rivalries were exacerbated. The world lurched toward World War II. As one American diplomat said at the end of World War II, "That bit of history was as well known in Cordell Hull's State Department as the Bible's account of the Fall of the Garden of Eden. History must not be repeated!"

To avoid that, the Allies, with the Soviet Union's grudging acquiescence, created the economic institutions known collectively as the Bretton Woods system. The World Bank, the International Monetary Fund, and the International Trade Organisation (this last did not materialise as the World Trade Organisation until much later) were designed to provide stability to the world's economy and to encourage free trade among nations. How much difference these all made to the international order after 1945 will always be a matter of debate, but the world did not get a repeat of the 1930s.

Memories of the Great Depression and the lessons to be learned from it came to the forefront again in the second half of 2008 as the world's financial system and then its economy lurched from one crisis to the next. Professional economists who had largely relegated John Maynard Keynes to the archives dusted off his works again, especially those parts where he talked of the need for government regulation of risk-taking and the obligations of governments to use the tools at their disposal to stimulate the economy. It was perhaps fortunate too that Benjamin S. Bernanke, the chairman of the Federal Reserve, one of the key figures in formulating American policy in those tense months, is an expert on the Depression. He has written and lectured extensively on what he sees as its lessons. In an article published in *Foreign Policy* in 2000, he argued that "the economic repercussions of a stock market crash depend less on the severity of the crash itself than on the response of economic policymakers, particularly central bankers". The Federal Reserve, he said, had been wrong in trying to protect the value of the dollar, by, for example raising interest rates, instead of trying to stabilise the domestic economy. In his reaction to the 2008 crisis, he was prepared to go further than many other officials in stimulating the economy.

In their book *Thinking in Time*, Richard Neustadt and Ernest May show how knowing the background to an issue can also help us avoid unnecessary and potentially costly mistakes. In the summer of 1979, to take their most telling example, rumours started to circulate that the Soviets had recently positioned combat troops in Cuba. Not only did this come at a time when relations between the Soviet Union and the United States were entering one of their tenser phases, but it brought back vivid memories of the Cuban missile crisis of 1962, when the Soviets had poured forces, including nuclear weapons, into Cuba. The crisis had ended when Khrushchev, bowing to demands from Kennedy, had withdrawn the rockets and nuclear weapons. Kennedy had given a quiet promise that, in turn, the United States would not invade Cuba. Was this Soviet brigade the start of a similar crisis, and what did the Soviets mean by apparently violating their agreement of 1962 to withdraw their troops?

President Carter's national security adviser, Zbigniew Brzezinski, asked the intelligence agencies to investigate. By the middle of August, reports had confirmed that there was a Soviet brigade in Cuba. Shortly thereafter, Senator Frank Church of Idaho, who was chair of the Senate Foreign Relations Committee, went public. "The president", he told reporters, "must make it clear, we draw the line on Russian penetration of this hemisphere". The crisis persisted through much of September. Gradually, two things emerged as the administration began to go back into the files. First, Kennedy had asked for the removal of Soviet ground troops but in the end had not insisted on it. Second, and this was particularly embarrassing, it appeared as though Soviet troops had been stationed in Cuba continuously since 1962. "Appallingly", wrote Cyrus Vance, Carter's secretary of state, "awareness of the Soviet ground force units had faded from the institutional memories of the intelligence agencies". Anatoly Dobrynin, the Soviet ambassador who had been in Washington since Kennedy's time, was in Moscow at his mother's deathbed. He rushed back to the United States to help sort out what was by now an increasingly dangerous crisis. In Moscow, his superiors had trouble believing that the whole fuss had been an honest mistake and speculated that the Americans must have very dark motives indeed. In Dobrynin's view, the whole farce led to the further deterioration of relations between the Soviet Union and the United States.

Two groups in particular in our society have always taken history seriously as a guide. People in business and in the military want to know what their chances of success are if they take a particular course of action. Will they lose their investment or, in the case of the military, the war? One way of narrowing the odds is to study similar situations in the past. That, after all, is what the case study is. Why was the Edsel a failure and the Volkswagen a success? In 2008, as the effects of the subprime mortgage crisis rippled through the world's economies, market analysts turned to history to try to determine how long the downturn in the stock markets would last. (In the past fifty years, apparently, we have had nine bear markets, and they have lasted on average just over a year.)

Investors may experience several bad patches; the military often never see a war, and it is the rare senior officer who fights in more than one. It is possible to practice war, in exercises, but those cannot replicate the actuality of war itself, with its real violence and death and all its confusion and unpredictability. So history becomes all the more important a tool for learning about possible reasons for victory and, equally important, for defeat. The weapons and uniforms are very different, yet military academies and staff colleges still find some utility in setting their students to studying the Peloponnesian Wars or Nelson's battles. After exercises and actual campaigns, the military study what happened and try to draw lessons from it. The official histories of World War II were meant to help governments and their military learn from successes and mistakes.

Today, some in the United States are trying to learn lessons to apply in Iraq from the war that France fought against Algerian nationalists from 1954 to 1962. There are indeed parallels: large, technologically advanced powers fighting an elusive yet ubiquitous enemy; a sullen civilian population, some of which gives active support to the insurgents; and Islam and nationalism fuelling the struggle. At the Marine Corps University in Virginia, young officers can now take a course on the French-Algerian War. The classic movie *The Battle of Algiers*, which shows the brutality on both sides, is being used in training by the Pentagon. "A little strange", said its left-wing Italian director, Gillo Pontecorvo, shortly before he died in 2006. "I think that the most that *The Battle of Algiers* can do is teach how to make cinema, not war." President Bush has been reading *A Savage War of Peace*, the classic account of the Algerian war. (On the Internet, copies were going for over $200 until the publisher rushed out a paperback.) In May 2007, Bush extended a rare invitation to stay in the White House to its British author, Alistair Horne. The president does not seem concerned that the French eventually lost their war. According to an aide, Bush found the book interesting but came to the conclusion that the French failed because their bureaucracy was not up to the job.

Paying attention to the past cannot always save the military from getting it wrong. Before World War I, there was plenty of evidence that the power of the defence was getting stronger. From the American Civil War to the Russo-Japanese War of 1904–5, the combination of trenches and greater and faster firepower was raising the cost of attack dramatically. Only a handful of observers took the trend seriously. Most European military thinkers discounted such wars on the grounds that they were being fought by less capable (in other words, non-European) forces. The French, predisposed by their own military history to think in terms of the offensive, found further consolation in the work of a young officer who had died in the first month of France's war with Prussia. Ardant du Picq argued that in the end victory came down to superior morale. French military planners also stressed superior firepower, better training and sheer weight of numbers, including cavalry, to carry the day. They paid very little attention in the years before 1914 to the techniques of defence. After 1918, they paid too much. The enormous losses of World War I, the long years of stalemate on the western front, and, above all, the desperate struggle around Verdun, where the French army held off the Germans, persuaded the French military and politicians that the future of war lay in the defence. Just when advances in airplanes, mobile artillery, tanks, and other motorised vehicles were making it possible to bypass or attack fortifications, the French sank their hopes and a good deal of their military budget into the Maginot Line. While much of the French army was waiting for the great German attack that never came, Hitler's forces were sweeping past the west end of the line.

By the end of the Vietnam War, the American military had learned a good deal about how to fight a counter-insurgency war against a nationalist movement that used both conventional and guerrilla forces. The only problem was that few people wanted to remember either Vietnam or its lessons. There was, said T. X. Hammes, a marine colonel who maintained an interest in counter-insurgency, "a pretty visceral reaction that we would not do this again". American military training focused on conventional war; counter-insurgency was not even mentioned in the army's core strategic planning in the 1970s. Hammes nevertheless studied the small wars in places such as Central America, Africa and Afghanistan and wrote a book on how to combat guerrilla warfare. A publisher turned it down: "Interesting book, well written, but a subject nobody's interested in because it's not going to happen". *The Sling and the Stone: On War in the 21st Century* finally came out in 2004 as the Americans were painfully learning in Iraq the lessons they had chosen to forget. In 2005, General David Petraeus, one of the few American generals to devise successful tactics in Iraq, set up a counter-insurgency academy there. Back in the United States, he made the study of counter-insurgency compulsory at the army's advanced training colleges. Two books, T. E. Lawrence's *Seven Pillars of Wisdom*, about the Arab revolt against the Turks during World War I, and *Counterinsurgency Warfare* by the French officer David Galula, became unexpected bestsellers in bookstores near army bases.

History can help us to be wise; it can also suggest to us what the likely outcome of our actions might be. There are no clear blueprints to be discovered in history that can help us shape the future as we wish. Each historical event is a unique congeries of factors, people or chronology. Yet by examining the past, we can get some useful lessons about how to proceed and some warning about what is or is not likely to happen. We do have to be careful to cast our gaze as widely as possible. If we look only for the lessons that reinforce decisions we have already made, we will run into trouble. In May 1941, as warnings poured in from all quarters that the Germans were getting ready to attack the Soviet Union, Stalin refused to listen to them. He did not want a war with Germany, because he knew just how ill prepared the Soviet Union was. And so he persuaded himself that Germany would not move until it had made peace with Great Britain. "Hitler and his generals are not so stupid as to fight at the same time on two fronts", Stalin told his inner circle. "That broke the neck of the Germans in the First World War." A month later, German troops overran the Soviet forces that had been told to take up defensive positions back from the borders. Stalin could have found other lessons from the past if he had wanted. Hitler had shown himself a gambler before when he had seized Austria and Czechoslovakia. His rapid and stunning victory over France in 1940 had served only to convince him that he was always right. Moreover, he had made no secret of his long-term goal of moving east to obtain territory for the German people.

History, if it is used with care, can present us with alternatives, help us to form the questions we need to ask of the present, and warn us about what might go wrong. In the 1920s, T. E. Lawrence criticised the British government for its involvement in what had become the new country of Iraq:

> The people of England have been led in Mesopotamia into a trap from which it will be hard to escape with dignity and honour. They have been tricked into it by a steady withholding of information. The Baghdad communiqués are belated, insincere, incomplete. Things

have been far worse than we have been told, our administration more bloody and inefficient than the public knows. It is a disgrace to our imperial record and may soon be too inflamed for any ordinary cure. We are today not far from a disaster. Our unfortunate troops, Indian and British, under hard conditions of climate and supply, are policing an immense area, paying dearly every day in lives for the willfully wrong policy of the civil administration in Baghdad but the responsibility, in this case, is not on the army which has acted only upon the request of the civil authorities.

In 2002, as the American and British governments prepared their plans for the swift invasion and what they confidently assumed would be a short occupation of Iraq, they would have been wise to look at that earlier occupation. The British had assumed then that it would be easy, that the locals would welcome them or at least remain quiescent, and that they would find an obliging Arab ruler to act as their proxy. Moreover, Iraq would pay for itself by exporting wheat and, possibly, the oil that was yet to be exploited. Those illusions barely lasted a year. In the summer of 1920, British forces were stretched to the limit as they tried to contain widespread revolts across the country. Although the British thought they had found their ruler in Faisal, whom they made king the following year, he never proved to be the compliant ruler they wanted. Iraq remained an uneasy and troublesome part of the British sphere of influence right up to the 1950s. Instead, the coalition looked at the wrong occupations – those of Germany and Japan after World War II – or perhaps it is fairer to say that the policy makers of 2002 took the wrong sorts of lessons from those episodes. President Bush confidently said in a speech to the American Enterprise Institute on February 26,

2003: "There was a time when many said that the cultures of Japan and Germany were incapable of sustaining democratic values. Well, they were wrong. Some say the same of Iraq today. They are mistaken." Yet those earlier occupations worked only because the Allies made thorough plans before their victory; they had thousands of troops on the ground; and they were dealing with an enemy that had admitted defeat.

If those making the crucial decisions in 2002 had wanted to know how Iraqis would respond to a foreign invasion and occupation, then they might have found some instructive ideas and warnings in the British experience there or in other occupations, such as the ones of Germany and Japan at the end of World War II. When we are trying to make sense of a situation (and may well have more information than we can absorb) and to come to a decision, we use analogies to try to discern a pattern and to sort out what is important from what is not. If President Bush or Prime Minister Blair decides that Saddam Hussein is rather like Hitler, then that suggests ways of dealing with him. If the economic crisis of 2008 is like the start of the Great Depression, then governments and central banks may decide to stimulate the economy. If it is more like the crash of the dot-com bubble in the 1990s, it may be wiser to treat it as a short-term correction in the markets. Human beings may not always get the right analogy, but they are almost certainly bound to try to use one.

The Chinese have understood this for centuries. Traditional Chinese civilisation invariably drew on the past for moral tales and examples of how to behave wisely. Even Chinese Communists, who represented a forward-looking ideology, could not escape the habits of centuries. Their leaders, from Mao down, repeatedly referred to events in the past, even the long distant past. It would be as though an American president or a Canadian prime minister casually slipped references to Julius Caesar or

Charlemagne into his conversations and expected his audiences to understand at once. When, at the end of the 1960s, Mao was contemplating opening up relations with the United States in part as a counterbalance to the Soviet Union, he had in mind the example of the statesman in the third century A.D. who had recommended allying with one of his country's two enemies to defeat the third – and who had urged his ruler to choose the power farther away as his ally on the grounds that it was dangerous to become too close to an enemy on one's borders. Seeing the results of Mao's decision – the expanding relationship between China and the United States and the increased respect with which the Soviet Union and then Russia treated China – it is hard to disagree with his reasoning.

When the United States led a coalition against Iraq in the Gulf War of 1991, its leaders had in mind two analogies. They did not want American forces to get bogged down inside the country as they had in Vietnam, and they wanted to deter Hussein's regime from further adventures as they had done with containment of the Soviet Union and the People's Republic of China in the Cold War. Although President George H. W. Bush and his chairman of the Joint Chiefs of Staff, General Colin Powell, were much criticised, especially by the Right, for not invading Iraq and deposing Hussein, in fact they acted wisely. American and coalition forces did not get bogged down in a land war, and although Hussein's regime survived, its capacity to threaten its neighbours was minimal. (It still, sadly, had the means to kill and repress Iraqi citizens.)

Analogies from history must, of course, be treated with care. Using the wrong one not only can present an oversimplified picture of a complex situation in the present but can lead to wrong decisions. After September 11, 2001, it became fashionable, especially among neoconservatives, to talk about how the West finds itself engaged in World War IV. Norman Podhoretz, a leading neocon thinker, argued that the Cold War was really World War III and that now, after a too-brief period of peace in the 1990s, we are engaged in an equally massive and deadly struggle against Islamic fundamentalism. As in the other world wars, the United States and its allies are the innocent party; others have thrust war upon them. The West is only defending itself, even in wars like the Iraq one where it launches an attack. In such a view, the war is a moral one, of good against bad. A convenient shorthand, the authorship of which is proudly claimed by the Canadian David Frum, is the "axis of evil". No matter that the Axis in World War II was a working set of alliances among Germany, Italy and Japan and that this one is said to include Iraq and Iran, countries that waged a long war against each other in the 1980s, and North Korea, whose leaders probably have trouble finding their two reputed partners on the map. No matter, too, that the Cold War was not like the great military struggles of the two world wars and ended not with an armistice on the battlefields but with the collapse of one of the protagonists. Those who criticise the open-ended and ill-defined nature of the "war on terror" or the occupation of Iraq are dismissed as isolationists, cowards, or worse. Reviewing Podhoretz's recent work, *World War IV: The Long Struggle Against Islamofascism,* Ian Buruma wrote: "The book expresses a weird longing for the state of war, for the clarity it brings, and for the chance to divide one's fellow citizens, or indeed the whole world, neatly into friends and foes, comrades and traitors, warriors and appeasers, those who are with us and those who are against."

Another analogy that has had a good airing over the years is Munich, shorthand for the appeasement policies the democracies used in the 1930s with the dictators in a vain effort to prevent another war. Named after the Munich conference of 1938, when Britain and France agreed that Hitler's Germany should have the German-speaking parts of Czechoslovakia, Munich has become the symbol of weakness in the face of aggression. If the democracies had stood up to Hitler, better still even earlier in the 1930s before Germany had rearmed, and to Italy and Japan, they could have prevented, so the critics of appeasement say, World War II. But what exactly does the analogy mean? That you should never talk to your enemies and try to find common ground? In that case, President Dwight Eisenhower when he talked to Nikita Khrushchev or Nixon with Mao might be described as appeasers. Was it wrong of the democracies in the 1930s to try to avoid war? They were haunted by the hideous death tolls in World War I, so very recently over, and by fears that the new technology of the bomber would destroy civilisation. Where men such as Neville Chamberlain were mistaken, and it is much easier to see in retrospect, was in believing that Hitler would stop once he satisfied Germany's "reasonable" goals such as *Anschluss* with Austria.

In May 2008, President Bush, in a speech to Israel's Knesset, attacked those who thought they could talk constructively with America's enemies such as Syria, Iran and the Hamas organisation. Although he did not name them, most people inferred that he meant President Jimmy Carter and the Democratic presidential candidate Barack Obama, and perhaps his hosts themselves. "As Nazi tanks crossed into Poland in 1939", Bush said, "an American senator declared: 'Lord, if only I could have talked to Hitler, all of this might have been avoided.' We have an obligation to call this what it is – the false comfort of appeasement, which has been repeatedly discredited by history." Yet are Syria and Iran the same as Nazi Germany? Is talking to them a sign of weakness or a sensible attempt to broker peace? Is it always wrong to talk to even terrorist organisations? The British fought

the IRA in Northern Ireland, but they were also willing to negotiate with them. What is appeasement and what is not is often not
clear-cut. What is undeniable is that the Munich analogy has had
a strong hold over statesmen and stateswomen ever since and has
been applied liberally to justify a whole range of policies. Anthony Eden, the British prime minister who succeeded Churchill,
employed the analogy to disastrous effect when he tried to deal
with Gamal Abdel Nasser, the Egyptian dictator, in 1956. Like
many leaders in what was then called the Third World, Nasser
was prepared to take assistance from both sides in the Cold War.
He bought arms from Communist Czechoslovakia but also tried
to get a loan from the United States to build the Aswan Dam on
the Nile. John Foster Dulles, the American secretary of state, was
unable to get the loan through Congress. In retaliation and to
raise the funds he needed, Nasser nationalised the Suez Canal,
which up to that point had been owned and managed by the
British. Eden's reaction was unequivocal. As British foreign secretary in the 1930s, he had dealt with dictators. Now he and the
world were facing the same thing again. As he wrote in his memoirs, "Success in a number of adventures involving the breaking
of agreements in Abyssinia, in the Rhineland, in Austria, in
Czechoslovakia, in Albania had persuaded Hitler and Mussolini
that democracies had not the will to resist, that they could march
with the certitude of success from signpost to signpost along the
road which led to world dominion ... As my colleagues and I sur-
veyed the scene in those autumn months of 1956, we were determined that the like should not come again". But Nasser was no
Hitler intent on conquering his neighbours. Rather, he was a nationalist who badly needed resources to develop his own country
and stake out a position of leadership in the Middle East. The
British action in collusion with the French and the Israelis to
seize the Suez Canal was not only badly conceived; it rallied the

Egyptians and the wider Arab world to Nasser's side. Furthermore, it infuriated the Americans, who, far from seeing a repeat of the 1930s, worried about the moral impact on other Third World countries.

In 1950, when North Korean troops moved into the South, President Harry Truman was clear about the need to take action: "Communism was acting in Korea just as Hitler and the Japanese had acted ten, fifteen, twenty years earlier." He may well have been right. There is no doubt that Stalin, like Hitler, was gambling on an easy victory; in Stalin's case, though, he was prepared to pull back his support for North Korea once it became too costly. There is little evidence that Hitler would have dropped his demands in Europe even in the face of stronger opposition from the democracies. He was determined upon war sooner or later. President Kennedy, whose senior thesis and then book, *Why England Slept*, was on British appeasement, had Munich in mind when he debated with his advisers how to deal with the Soviet Union over its missiles in Cuba. The 1930s, Kennedy said, "taught us a clear lesson; aggressive conduct, if allowed to go unchecked and unchallenged, ultimately leads to war". Wisely, though, he used a naval blockade rather than outright war to put pressure on the Soviets. Fortunately, too, he had just read Barbara Tuchman's book *The Guns of August*, on the outbreak of World War I, and he was painfully aware of how a series of mistakes and blunders can produce a major catastrophe. A few years later Kennedy's successor, Lyndon Johnson, again used the analogy, this time with Vietnam. He did not want to be like Neville Chamberlain, the British prime minister who dealt with Hitler. He knew that if he got out of Vietnam, he told his biographer, "I'd be giving a big fat reward to aggression".

When Johnson had to decide whether or not to commit ground troops to Vietnam in 1965, the debate within his administration relied heavily on analogies. As Yuen Foong Khong of Oxford University has shown, Munich, the Korean War, and the French defeat in 1954 all were called in to support what were intense arguments. On the one hand were those like Robert McNamara; Dean Rusk, the secretary of state; and William Bundy, the assistant secretary of state for East Asian and Pacific Affairs who argued that both Munich and Korea encouraged a greater American presence in Vietnam. As Bundy put it, the lesson was that "aggression of any sort must be met early and head-on or it will have to be met later and in tougher circumstances. We had relearned the lessons of the 1930s – Manchuria, Ethiopia, the Rhineland, Czechoslovakia." What they had also learned, and this complicated the decision, was that China was likely to intervene if war came too close to its borders. That, in the end, was to limit the American response in Vietnam in a way that it had not been limited in Korea.

The most prominent advocate against sending the troops was George Ball, an undersecretary of state. In the spring of 1965 he warned that even with half a million troops, the United States "may *not* be able to fight the war successfully enough". The analogy he used was the French war in Vietnam, which had ended with the surrender of its garrison at Dien Bien Phu. "The French", he pointed out, "fought a war in Viet-nam [*sic*], and were fully defeated – after seven years of bloody struggle and when they still had 250,000 combat-hardened veterans in the field, supported by an army of 205,000 South Vietnamese". He also warned that in the eyes of many Vietnamese, the Americans had simply replaced the French as the colonial power. Like President Bush was to do later with the analogy between Algeria and Iraq, Ball's adversaries concentrated on showing where the Americans were different from the French. France had been divided over the war, and its political leadership was weak and unstable. The

American public generally supported the war, except for a few clergymen and academics, and the administration was determined to stay in and win. Furthermore, most "knowledgable" Vietnamese knew that the United States was there not for its own selfish ends but to defend the independence of South Vietnam. In the battle of the analogies, Ball lost. As Henry Cabot Lodge, the American ambassador in South Vietnam, said to great effect, "I feel there is a greater threat to start World War III if we don't go in. Can't you see the similarity to our own indolence at Munich?"

The Vietnam War in turn was to produce its own set of analogies. Two main ways of drawing lessons came out of that unhappy experience. The lesson that tended to find favour with liberals and Democrats but also with parts of the military was that the United States should never have got involved in the first place. Eisenhower, Kennedy, and then Johnson had allowed the United States to slide into a war without clearly defined aims and where crucial American interests did not appear to be at stake. The result had been a loss of moral authority for the United States as it increasingly found itself cast as an imperialist bully and as its soldiers committed atrocities such as the massacre at My Lai. The important lesson was that the United States should avoid getting drawn into such conflicts again. The other lesson, more appealing to the Right, was that the war in Vietnam could have been won if only the United States had been prepared to go all out, bombing North Vietnam into submission and putting even more troops on the ground. The press and public opinion should have been managed better to prevent the sort of sniping and defeatism that had undermined the war effort at home.

In 1991, as the Bush Sr. administration contemplated taking action against Hussein, Vietnam came into play as an example of how not to do it. Colin Powell, who had fought in Vietnam, had been drawing lessons ever since. If the United States ever fought another war, it should go in with overwhelming force and with clear goals. It should never again get drawn into an open-ended conflict that bled the armed forces and created dissent at home. Munich was part of the justification. Certainly, in his invasion of Kuwait, Hussein was the undoubted aggressor, and military action did stop any further attempts at meddling with his neighbours. Iraq was left severely weakened and willing to cooperate, if grudgingly, with United Nations arms inspectors.

When the new Bush administration focused on Iraq after September 11, it, too, used the Munich analogy, but its relevance was much more tenuous. In the 1930s, Hitler headed one of the most powerful countries in the world. As the American scholar Jeffrey Record put it, "Hitler was neither weak nor deterred; Saddam was nothing but weak and deterred". In 1991, Operation Desert Storm was over almost before it started. In 2003, it took three weeks to defeat Hussein completely with a relatively small force; it had taken four years to defeat Hitler with the combined forces of the British Empire, the Soviet Union and the United States. Although both the Bush and the Blair administrations tried to portray Hussein as a menace to the world in the lead-up to the invasion, their evidence, as we now know, that he possessed weapons of mass destruction was flimsy at best. And the assertion that Hussein was somehow allied with Osama bin Laden was absurd to anyone who knew history. Hussein was a secularist, bin Laden a religious fanatic. There had been no love lost between the two men, and indeed bin Laden had repeatedly called upon Iraqis to overthrow Hussein. We can learn from history, but we also deceive ourselves when we selectively take evidence from the past to justify what we have already made up our minds to do.

Conclusion

On the evening of September 11, 2001, the American writer Susan Jacoby overheard two men talking in a New York bar. "This is just like Pearl Harbor", one said. "What is Pearl Harbor?" the other asked. "That was when the Vietnamese dropped bombs in a harbour, and it started the Vietnam War", the first man replied. Does it matter that they got it so wrong? I would argue that it does, that a citizenry that cannot begin to put the present into context, that has so little knowledge of the past, can too easily be fed stories by those who claim to speak with the knowledge of history and its lessons. History is called in, as we have seen, to strengthen group solidarity, often at the expense of the individual, to justify treating others badly, and to bolster arguments for particular policies and courses of action. Knowledge of the past helps us to challenge dogmatic statements and sweeping generalisations. It helps us all think more clearly.

If those two bewildered men in the bar had known about Pearl Harbor, they would have understood that the attack on the World Trade Center was not the same as Japan attacking the United States in 1941. That was a war between two states; this was an act of terrorism. That in turn suggested that the tactics and strategy would have to be different from before. Although many, including the Bush administration, talked about a war on terror, the analogy was misleading. Wars are made on enemies, not on ideas; wars have defined goals – usually forcing the enemy to capitulate – but a war on terror has no clearly defined end. Nor was the attack on the World Trade Center anything like Vietnam. There the United States was carrying the war to the enemy's country, and, again, it had a solid enemy in North Vietnam and its southern allies.

In the aftermath of September 11, when Americans were shocked, angry and frightened, it was crucial that they and their leaders be able to think clearly. Who, to begin with, was the enemy? Here history was helpful because it cast light not only on Al Qaeda and its goals but on the reasons for its anger at the West. History was also there to remind Americans of how their country tended to behave in the world and in the face of threats. Those reminders were largely ignored by the administration as it prepared for war on first Afghanistan and then Iraq. A year after the attack on the World Trade Center, Paul Schroeder, one of the most thoughtful of the United States' historians of foreign affairs, wrote an article, "What Has Changed Since 9/11? Not Much, and Not for the Better," in which he urged Americans to put what had happened in a larger historical and global context. Yes, he said, the attack had been frightful, but it had not done long-term damage to the United States. True, the terrorist threat remained a serious one, but it was not as great as those suffered by other states in the present and in the past. Yet the Bush administration was using September 11 to claim the right for the United States to decide whom to attack when it pleased without consulting its allies or world bodies such as the United Nations. "It is hard to grasp and impossible to exaggerate", Schroeder wrote, "how novel, sweeping, dangerous, and subversive of world order and peace this new Bush doctrine is. It violates the two foundation stones of the international system developed over the last five centuries: the principle of the independence, juridical equality, and coordinate status of its component units (now almost entirely states), and its equally vital counter principle, the need and requirement for such independent units to form and join associations for common purposes and to follow recognised norms and practices, especially in seeking peace and security". The United States, moreover, was abandoning its own history of working with others to uphold a world order and, in its invasion and occupation of Iraq, its long history of opposition to imperialism. Worse, as Abu Ghraib and Guantánamo would show, it was going to undermine and compromise its own deep respect for the rule of law.

History, by giving context and examples, helps when it comes to thinking about the present world. It aids in formulating questions, and without good questions it is difficult to begin to think in a coherent way at all. Knowledge of history suggests what sort of information might be needed to answer those questions. Experience teaches how to assess that information. As they look at the past, historians learn to behave rather like the examining magistrate in the French judicial system. What happened and why? the historian asks. History demands that we treat evidence seriously, especially when that evidence contradicts assumptions we have already made. Are the witnesses telling the truth? How do we weigh one version against another? Have we been asking the right or the only questions? Historians go further and ask what a particular event, thought or attitude from the past signifies. How important is it? The answers in part will depend on what we in the present ask and what we think is important. History does not produce definitive answers for all time. It is a process.

History can help us to make sense of a complicated world, but it also warns of the dangers of assuming that there is only one possible way of looking at things or only one course of action. We must always be prepared to consider alternatives and to raise objections. We should not be impressed when our leaders say firmly, "History teaches us" or "History will show that we were right". They can oversimplify and force inexact comparisons just as much as any of us can. Even the very clever and the powerful (and the two are not necessarily the same) go confidently off down the wrong paths. It is useful, too, to be reminded, as a citizen, that those in positions of authority do not always know better.

Because history relies on a sceptical frame of mind, whether toward evidence or comprehensive explanations, it can also inculcate a healthy propensity to question our leaders. They are not always right, indeed often the opposite. In 1893, the British naval commander in the Mediterranean, Vice Admiral George Tryon, decided to take personal command of the summer naval manoeuvres. When he ordered an about-face of two parallel rows of battleships, his officers tried to point out that there would be a collision. A relatively simple calculation demonstrated that the combined turning circles of the ships were greater than the distance between them. While his officers watched in dismay, his flagship, *Victoria*, was rammed by the *Camperdown*. Tryon refused to believe that the damage was serious and ordered the nearby vessels not to send their lifeboats. The *Victoria* sank, taking him and 357 sailors with it. The Charge of the Light Brigade, when the flower of the British cavalry rode straight into the mouths of the Russian guns, is an equal reminder of human folly, not just of Lord Cardigan, who led the charge, but of the system that allowed him to be in command. As David Halberstam, the American journalist, said in the last piece he ever wrote, "It is a story from the past we read again and again, that the most dangerous time for any nation may be that moment in its history when things are going unusually well, because its leaders become carried away with hubris and a sense of entitlement cloaked as rectitude".

Humility is one of the most useful lessons the past can provide the present. As John Carey, the distinguished British man of letters, puts it, "One of history's most useful tasks is to bring home to us how keenly, honestly and painfully, past generations pursued aims that now seem to us wrong or disgraceful". Slavery once had its defenders. Think of the arguments over the position of the earth and the sun, of the conviction, apparently supported by science, that so many Victorians had that there were superior and inferior races, or the calm assumptions even a few decades ago that women and blacks could not make good engineers or doctors.

History also encourages people in the present to reflect on themselves. "The past is a foreign country; they do things differently there", the English novelist L. P. Hartley once wrote. Knowing that classical Chinese civilisation valued scholars above soldiers or that the Roman family was very different from the nuclear one of the modern West suggests other values and other ways of organising society. That is not to say that all values are relative; rather, we should be prepared to examine our own and not merely take them for granted as somehow being the best. John Arnold, the British historian, put it elegantly: "Visiting the past is something like visiting a foreign country: they do some things the same and some things differently, but above all else they make us more aware of what we call 'home'."

If the study of history does nothing more than teach us humility, scepticism, and awareness of ourselves, then it has done something useful. We must continue to examine our own assumptions and those of others and ask, where's the evidence? Or, is there another explanation? We should be wary of grand claims in history's name or those who claim to have uncovered the truth once and for all. In the end, my only advice is use it, enjoy it, but always handle history with care.

ACKNOWLEDGMENTS

This book grew out of an invitation I received from the History Department at the University of Western Ontario to give the Joanne Goodman lectures in the fall of 2007. The series, named in memory of a history student who was tragically killed in a car accident, date back to 1966 and have had a distinguished roster of lecturers. It was an honour to be among their number and also a wonderful opportunity to reflect on a subject of my own choosing. I am grateful to the faculty and students at Western who sat through my lectures and helped me to refine my thinking through their questions and comments.

I was very lucky to have found in Jonathan Weier an outstanding research assistant who in the end became more of a collaborator. I am also grateful, as always, to those friends and family who discussed my ideas with me and who read my drafts with such patience. They make a long list but I should single out for special mention my brothers Tom and David; my sister Ann; my brother-in-law Peter Snow; and my nephews Dan and Alex; as well as my agent Caroline Dawnay and her Canadian counterpart Michael Levine. My mother, Eluned, as usual was an excellent critic and proofreader. Bob Bothwell has taught me so much about history over the years that it is difficult to thank him adequately. Yet again, he was kind enough to read my manuscript and give me his advice. I have also benefited greatly from being at Oxford University and talking to my many new colleagues who are interested in the ways in which history is used. I owe particular thanks to Anne Deighton, Rosemary Foot, Yuen Foong Khong, Kalypso Nicholaïdis, and Avi Shlaim and also to the students at St Antony's who have patiently listened to me talk and sent me much valuable information. Finally, but not last, are those at Profile who brought this book into being: Andrew Franklin and Ruth Killick. Thank you.

FURTHER READING

There is a large and growing literature on the uses and abuses of both history and memory. The following is a list of some of the works I found most useful.

Abu El-Haj, Nadia. *Facts on the Ground: Archaeological Practice and Territorial Self-Fashioning in Israeli Society*. Chicago: University of Chicago Press, 2002.

Appleby, R. Scott. "History in the Fundamentalist Imagination". *Journal of American History* 89, no. 2 (2002).

Arnold, John H. *History: A Very Short Introduction*. Oxford: Oxford University Press, 2000.

Bacevich, Andrew J. "The Real World War IV". *Wilson Quarterly* 29, no. 1 (Winter 2005).

Bell, Duncan, ed. *Memory, Trauma, and World Politics: Reflections on the Relationship Between Past and Present*. Basingstoke, U.K: Palgrave Macmillan, 2006.

Black, Jeremy. *The Curse of History*. London: Social Affairs Unit, 2008.

Brundage, W. Fitzhugh. *The Southern Past*. Cambridge, Mass.: Harvard University Press, 2005.

Cannadine, David, ed. *What Is History Now?* Basingstoke, U.K.: Palgrave Macmillan, 2002.

Carr, E. H. *What Is History?* London: Macmillan, 1961.

Collingwood, R. G. *The Idea of History.* Rev. ed. Oxford: Oxford University Press, 1994.

Delisle, Esther. *Myths, Memory, and Lies: Quebec's Intelligentsia and the Fascist Temptation, 1939–1960.* Westmount, Q.C.: Robert Davies, 1998.

Evans, Richard. *In Defence of History.* London: Granta, 2000.

Fischer, David Hackett. *Historians' Fallacies: Toward a Logic of Historical Thought.* New York: Harper and Row, 1970.

Gardner, Lloyd C., and Marilyn B. Young. *Iraq and the Lessons of Vietnam; or, How Not to Learn from the Past.* New York: New Press, 2007.

Geary, Patrick J. *The Myth of Nations: The Medieval Origins of Europe.* Princeton, N.J.: Princeton University Press, 2002.

Gillis, John R., ed. *Commemorations: The Politics of National Identity.* Princeton, N.J.: Princeton University Press, 1994.

Halberstam, David. "The History Boys". *Vanity Fair,* Aug. 2007.

History & Memory (journal).

Hobsbawm, Eric, and Terence Ranger. *The Invention of Tradition.* Cambridge, U.K.: Cambridge University Press, 1983.

Howard, Michael. *Captain Professor: The Memoirs of Sir Michael Howard.* London: Continuum, 2006.

——— . "The Use and Abuse of Military History." *RUSI Journal* 107 (Feb. 1962).

Judah, Tim. *The Serbs: History, Myth, and the Destruction of Yugoslavia.* New Haven, Conn.: Yale University Press, 1997.

Karlsson, Klas-Göran, and Ulf Zander, eds. *Echoes of the Holocaust: Historical Cultures in Contemporary Europe.* Lund, Sweden: Nordic Academic Press, 2003.

Khong, Yuen Foong. *Analogies at War: Korea, Munich, Dien Bien Phu, and the Vietnam Decisions of 1965.* Princeton, N.J.: Princeton University Press, 1992.

Lebow, Richard Ned, Wulf Kansteiner, and Claudio Fogu, eds. *The Politics of Memory in Postwar Europe.* Durham, N.C.: Duke University Press, 2006.

Linenthal, Edward T., and Tom Engelhardt. *History Wars: The Enola Gay and Other Battles for the American Past.* New York: Henry Holt, 1996.

Lowenthal, David. *The Heritage Crusade and the Spoils of History.* Cambridge, U.K.: Cambridge University Press, 1998.

May, Ernest R. *"Lessons" of the Past: The Use and Misuse of History in American Foreign Policy.* New York: Oxford University Press, 1973.

Murray, Williamson, and Richard Hart Sinnreich. *The Past as Prologue: The Importance of History to the Military Profession.* Cambridge, U.K.: Cambridge University Press, 2006.

Neustadt, Richard E., and Ernest R. May. *Thinking in Time: The Uses of History for Decision Makers.* New York: Free Press, 1986.

Nobles, Melissa. *The Politics of Official Apologies.* New York: Cambridge University Press, 2008.

Novick, Peter. *The Holocaust in American Life.* Boston: Houghton Mifflin, 2000.

Pappé, Ilan. *The Ethnic Cleansing of Palestine.* London: Oneworld, 2006.

Record, Jeffrey. "The Use and Abuse of History: Munich, Vietnam, and Iraq". *Survival* 49, no. 1 (Spring 2007).

Winter, Jay. *Remembering War: The Great War Between Memory and History in the Twentieth Century.* New Haven, Conn.: Yale University Press, 2006.

Winter, Jay, and Antoine Prost. *The Great War in History: Debates and Controversies, 1914 to the Present.* Cambridge, U.K.: Cambridge University Press, 2005.

Yoshida, Takashi. *The Making of the "Rape of Nanking": History and Memory in Japan, China, and the United States.* New York: Oxford University Press, 2006.

INDEX

A

Abu El-Haj, Nadia 109
   Facts on the Ground 107
Abu Ghraib prison, Iraq 167
Abyssinia (later Ethiopia) 160
Acheson, Dean 45
Adenauer, Konrad 133
Adwan, Sami 137
Afghanistan 153
   American preparation for war on
      166
   Canada's campaign in 66, 125
   shown as capable of being
      conquered 146
Africa
   American slaves' descendants and
      DNA decoding 7
   small wars in 153
African American history 56, 57, 59–60
African American Lives (PBS television
   program) 7
African history 56
African National Congress 25
Air Ministry (British) 41
Akbar, Mogul emperor 76
Al Qaeda 129, 166
Albania, Albanians 62, 88, 105, 160
Alexander the Great 146
Alexandria 73
Alsace 101, 102
Amazon website 109
America, Richard 30

American Air Force Association 124
American Civil War (1861–5) xii, 56,
   57, 117, 152
American Enterprise Institute 155
American West, myth of the 55–6
Anderson, Benedict 54, 81
Anglican Church 58
Anschluss (1938) 134, 154, 159
anti-Semitism 69
apartheid 25–6, 107
apologies
   apologies to indiginous peoples
      24–25, 26, 29–30
   apologies for war crimes 24, 28, 30
   apologies for past policies 25–26,
      26–27, 28, 29, 30
appeasement 158–60, 161
Arandora Star, sinking of (1940) 28
Armenia, Armenians 10, 97, 120
Army Corps of Engineers 71
army regiments 54
Arnold, John 169
Arthur, King 116
Aryans
   Aryan movement into India 74, 77
   and Harappan civilization 74
   and Hindu nationalists 74
Ashe, Arthur 57
Asia
   China's claims to leadership in 96
   new economic powers in 9
Aswan Dam 160

Atatürk, Kemal 63, 65
Athens 73
Augustus Caesar, Emperor 3
Aussaresses, General Paul 129
Austerlitz, Battle of (1805) 129
Australia
    Aborginal communities 29–30, 115, 122
    contested story of arrival of first whites 136
    explorers and entrepreneurs 122–3
    Howard tries to promote a national history curriculum 136
    internment in 28
    National Museum 122–3
    Stolen Generations of Aboriginal children 29, 30, 115
Austria 160
    amnesia about its Nazi past 134–5
    Anschluss (1938) 134, 154, 159
    Austrian "enemy aliens" in Britain 28
    and destruction of the Jews 135
    part in the destruction of the Jews 135
    portrays itself as first victim of Nazism 134
    questions about Austria's role (from 1960s) 135
Austria-Hungary 27, 81, 84, 102
Austrian Empire 93
authoritarian regimes 67
"axis of evil" 158
Ayodhya mosque, northern India 74

B
Babcock, John 19
baby boom generation 38
Baker, Kenneth 115–16
Balkans, the 10, 11, 88, 103, 146
Ball, George 162, 163
Banat, the 104
Bar-On, Dan 137
Barbie, Klaus (the "Butcher of Lyon") 130
Barnard College, New York 109
Bataan death march (1942) 124

Battle of Algiers, The (film) 151
battle honors 54
Beijing
    burning of Summer Palace (1860) 95
    Forbidden City 23
    top Chinese leaders located in 8
Belarus 103
Ben-Gurion, David 105, 109
Ben-Yair, Elazar 48
Berlin
    Holocaust memorial 134
    Kaiser Wilhelm Memorial Church 134
    National Memorial for the Victims of War and Tyranny 134
Berlin airlift (1948–9) 21
Bernanke, Benjamin S. 148–9
Berthier, Ferdinand 61
Bethlehem University 137
Betjeman, Sir John 267
Beyond the Fringe (satirical review): "Aftermyth of War" sketch 42
Bharatiya Janata Party (BJP) 74–6, 78
Billy the Kid 55
bin Laden, Osama 65, 164
Biological Psychiatry Lab, McLean Hospital 46
Black Cultural Centre, Nova Scotia 60
Black History Month (Canada) 60
Black History Month (United States) 59
blacks, perceived inferiority of 169
Blair, Tony 26, 145, 156, 164
Boadicea (Boudica) 116
Boer War (1899–1901) 146
Bolshevik Revolution (1917) 64, 65, 131
Bolsheviks 23
Bombay 100
Bosnia 10
Bosnian Muslims 87, 94
Bourbons 8
Brandt, Willy 137
Bretton Woods system 148
Britain
    history education 115–16
    imperialism 15–16

internment of German subjects 28
and Munich conference (1938) 159
official histories of World War II
  40–41
posthumous pardoning of soldiers
  executed for cowardice (World
  War I) 27
and the Suez crisis 160–61
Britain's Deaf Heritage 60
British Empire 11, 116, 128, 164
British Museum 123
Brook, Sir Norman 41
Brown, Gordon 116–17
Brown University, Providence, Rhode
  Island 30
Brzezinski, Zbigniew 149
Buchanan, Pat 124–5
Bulgarians 103
Bullitt, William 36
Bundy, William 162
Burma 95
Burns, Ken: documentaries 4
Buruma, Ian 158
Bush, George H. W. 64, 118, 157, 163
Bush, George W. 55, 118
  and the Algerian war 151–2, 162
  and Churchill 17
  low ratings 20
  and occupations of Germany and
    Japan 155–6
  "Preserve America" executive order
    (2003) 5–6
  and Truman 20, 21–2
  untimely use of word "crusade"
    145
  war on terror 66
  weapons of mass destruction issue
    164
Butler, Sir James 40

C
Caernarfon Castle 85
Caesar, Julius 156
caliphate, the 64, 65
Camp David negotiations 107
Camperdown (ship) 168
Canaanites 107, 108

Canada
  conditions on reserves 31
  Conquest of Quebec (1759) xii
  disputes over public holidays 127–8
  French Canadian nationalists xii,
    68–9
  head tax on Chinese immigrants
    26–7
  "heritage" 4
  internees 27–8
  land disputes by aboriginals 104–5
  Native land 100
  Ottawa War Museum 125–7
  residential schools 30–31
  self-perception as a benevolent
    force in the world 146
  Supreme Court 126
  Toronto terrorist plot 114
  World War I veterans 18–19
Canada Day (previously Dominion
  Day) 128
Canadian army: troops in Afghanistan
  66
Canadian Broadcasting Corporation
  126
Canadian House of Commons
  and state funerals for last Canadian
    veterans 18–19
  and *The Valour and the Horror* series
    126
Canadian War Museum 125–7
  Allied bombing of Germany exhibit
    42, 44
Canterbury, archbishop of 85
capitalism 38, 134, 142, 143–4
  liberal 9
Cardigan, Lord 168
Carey, John 169
Caroline, Queen 85
Carter, Jimmy 144, 149, 159
Carthage 147
Castro, Fidel 44–5
Catherine of Braganza 100
Catholic Church 39, 130
Catholicism 82, 93
causality 38
Celil, Huseyin 96

Central America, small wars in 153
Chadderton, Cliff 127
Châlons-sur-Marne, France 5
Chamberlain, Neville 159, 161
Charge of the Light Brigade (1854) 168
Charlemagne 157
Charles, HRH The Prince of Wales
    100
Charles II, King 100
Chávez, Hugo 128
Cheney, Dick 118
Cheney, Lynne 118
Chicago World's Fair (1893) 5
Chile 136
Chimneypot Preservation and
    Protection Society 4
China
    attack on Japanese businesses 96–7
    Century of Humiliation 68, 95
    challenges United States 11
    claims to leadership in Asia 96
    Communism 8, 17, 156
    as an escape from the present 16
    expanding relationship with United
        States 157
    Great Wall 67–8
    and Hindu warriors 75
    history as a dynastic cycle 16
    history rewritten in 23
    influence on Japanese culture 70
    invasion and occupation of Tibet
        104
    Japanese invasion of (1937) 68, 135
    leaders' repeated references to the
        past 156
    museums devoted to Japanese
        atrocities of World War II 4, 123
    new textbooks 121–2
    Nixon's initiative 22, 67
    Patriotic Education 67, 96
    Qin Emperor (Qin Shi Huang) 17,
        23–4
    relations with Japan 96
    scholars valued above soldiers in
        classical Chinese civilization 169
    Shanghai park story 4, 95
    Sino-Soviet split 143
    and Taiwan 104
    triumph of Communists (1949) 95,
        143
Chinese Canadians 26–7
Chinese Communist Party 67, 68, 95,
    97, 121, 122
    Politburo 67
Chirac, Jacques 18, 131
Christianity, Christians
    conflicts with Muslims 9
    in India 75
    and the Serbs 93
Church, Senator Frank 149–50
Churchill, Sir Winston 17, 18, 40, 43,
    88, 103, 143, 160
Ciampi, Carlo Azeglio 19
citizenship 101
civil rights movement 57
Clark, Mark 147
Clinton, Bill 19, 26, 107, 118, 144
Clinton, Hillary 94
Cold War 9, 10, 11, 21, 22, 45, 121, 134,
    142, 157, 158, 160
collective memory 48, 49, 81
College of Arms, London 6
Collingwood, R. G. 43
colonialism 68, 105, 129, 136, 146
Columbia River 71
Columbus, Christopher 128
Columbus Day (United States) 128
Communism 81, 142
    Chinese 8, 95, 143
    and Korea 161
    and "scientific" history 15
    Soviet 8, 9, 23
Communist Revolution 67
company heads, lack of trust in 19
Congo River 100
Conservative Party 116
Conservatives: escaping from the
    present 16
Cornwall, Duchy of 100
coronations 85
counterinsurgency 153
Croatia 88, 93
Croats 87
    conflicts with Serbs 9, 88

history of 68
view of their past 93
Cromwell, Oliver 132
Crusades 26, 64, 66, 145
Cuba
    crisis of 1979 149–50
    missile crisis (1962) 9, 142–3, 149
"cultural genocide" 31
Cultural Revolution 67, 136
cultural studies 37
Cyrus the Great, King of Persia 17
Czechoslovakia 102, 154, 159, 160, 162

D
Da Vinci Code, The (Brown) 73
Dalai Lama 95, 104
Darius the Great, King of Persia 17
David, King 108
Day of Accord and Reconciliation
    (Russia) 131
Day of National Unity (Russia) 131
de Klerk, Frederik Willem 25
deaf activists 60, 61
*Deaf Heritage in Canada: A Distinctive,
    Diverse, and Enduring Culture* 60
Deaf history 61
deaf people 60–61
democracy 101, 132, 144
    liberal 10
Democrats (US) 22, 163
Deng Xiaoping 95
Department of Canadian Heritage 4
Deslisle, Esther 69
dictators
    attempt to rewrite history 22–3
    efforts to ensure their own
        immortality 23–4
Dien Bien Phu garrison, Vietnam
    162
Dilke, Sir Charles 15–16
Dinur, Ben-Zion 89, 106
Diop, Cheikh Anta 73
Dmowski, Roman 103
DNA decoding 7–8
Dobrynin, Anatoly 150
Dolci, Danilo 83
Dole, Senator Bob 119

Dominion Day (renamed Canada Day)
    128
Dominion Institute, Canada 18, 19, 115
Doniger, Professor Wendy 77
dot-com bubble (1990s) 156
Dulles, John Foster 95, 160
Duncan Smith, Iain 19
Dunkirk, Battle of (1940) 84
Dusan, Prince 86

E
East Germany
    avoids its Nazi past 134
    opposition to Fascism 134
Easter Rising (1916) 72
"ecocide" 128
economic crisis (2008) 149, 150, 156
Eden, Sir Anthony (later 1st Earl of
    Avon) 160
Edsel car 150
Edward VIII, King (as Prince of Wales)
    85
Egypt 106, 108
    ancient 73
Eichmann, Adolf: trial in Jerusalem
    (1961) 133
Einstein, Albert 118
Eisenhower, Dwight 159, 163
Elizabeth I, Queen 4, 85
Elizabeth II, Queen: apologises to
    Maori of New Zealand 24
Enola Gay (B-29 bomber) 123
ethnic groups 8
ethnic nationalism 11
ethnography 102, 103
European empires, disappearance of 38
European Union 65, 97

F
Faisal, King of Saudi Arabia 155
Fallaci, Oriana 55
Fascism 11, 16, 63–4, 69, 81, 134
fatwa 77
Federal Reserve 148, 149
feminists 59
Festival of the Planet's Tribes parade
    (Paris, 1989) 129

Feuerstein, Wolfgang 90
Figl, Leopold 134
Filion, Gérard 69
Fischer, David Hackett 55
Ford, Gerald 59–60
Ford, Henry xii
Foreign Office (British) 145
Foreign Policy 149
Founding Fathers 117
Fourteen Points 98
Fraga, Manuel 132
France
    Année du Patrimoine (1980) 4–5
    Chirac's admission 131
    claims the Rhineland 82
    conflicts with Germans 9
    falls to the Nazis (1940) 40, 154
    Franco-Prussian War (1870–71) 101
    joint history textbook with
      Germany (2006) 137
    Ministry of Culture 4
    and Munich conference (1938) 159
    Muslim immigrants 114
    National Assembly 130
    revisiting the past 5
    and significance of French
      Revolution 129
    Vichy government 69, 130–31
    and Vietnam War 162
    World War I veterans 18
Franco, General Francisco 132
Franco-Prussian War (1870–71) 101
Frank, Anne: *The Diary of Anne Frank* 133
Frankland, Noble 41–2, 43
Franz Joseph, Emperor of Austria 28
Frederick the Great, King of Prussia 64
    two hundredth anniversary of his
      death 128–9
Frederick I Barbarossa, Holy Roman
    Emperor 64
Free French 130
Freezing Point (journal) 121
French army 129, 152
French Resistance 130
French Revolution (1789–99) 8, 38
    two-hundredth anniversary of
      (1989) 5, 129

French television 131
French-Algerian War (1954–62) 129,
    151–2, 162
Freud, Sigmund 36, 46
Friends Reunited 6
Frum, David 158
Fukuyama, Francis 10

G
Gaddis, John Lewis 141
Galileo Galilei 3
Gallipoli landings (1915) 17
Galula, David: *Counterinsurgency Warfare*
    153
Gambia 26
Garašanin, Ilija 87
Garvey, Marcus: "Who and What Is a
    Negro?" 72–3
Gaulle, General Charles de 130
gays
    gay activists 59
    gay history 59
    gay rights movement 38
    oppression and victimization of 59
Gaza 94, 106
Geist (infinite spirit) 15
genealogy 6–8
Geneva conference (1954) 95
Genghis Khan 8, 146
genocide 122, 128, 136
George IV, King 85
Georgetown University 30
Georgia 10
German army, and Serbia (World War
    II) 146
Germany
    Allied bombing campaign 41–5,
      125–7
    birth of new Germany 101
    brought into being by nationalism
      81
    challenges British Empire for
      hegemony 11
    compensation to Jewish families 24
    conflicts with the French 9
    confronts its Nazi past 133–4
    defeat in World War I 98, 102

drops out of League of Nations 147
fights on two fronts in World War I
    154
financial problems of 1920s 37
folktales 83
Foreign Ministry 99
German "enemy aliens" in Britain
    28
invasion of Poland (1939) 159
joint history textbook with France
    (2006) 137
memoirs by concentration camp
    survivors 133
memorials and concentration camp
    museums 133–4
monarchy vanishes 98
Nazi 16, 28
occupation at end of World War II
    147, 155–6
an organic German nation 15
origins of German nation 83
post-war preoccupation with
    survival and rebuilding 133
reparations 37, 98, 99
silence about the past 133
and Treaty of Versailles 97–9
Gettysburg, Battle of (1863) 84
Gibbon, Edward 141
glasnost 138
Glenny, Misha 10
globalization 53
Golan Heights 106
Golwalkar, Madhav 74
Gorbachev, Mikhail 138
Gorton, Senator Slade 119
gossip, craze for 19–20
Goths 84
Gow, Andrew Colin 35–6
grand patterns 15–16
Great Depression 37, 148–9
Great Wall of China 67–8
Greco-Turkish War (1919–22) 62–3
Greek civilization 62, 73
Greek language 62
Grey, Zane 55
Griffiths, Rudyard 19
Grimm brothers 83

Groulx, Abbé Lionel 69
groups 54, 58–9
Guantánamo, Cuba 167
guerrilla warfare 153
Gulag, the 132, 138
Gulf Institute 24
Gulf War (1991) 65, 157
Gunsmoke (television series) 55
Gush Emunim 107
Gypsies 134

H
Haaretz newspaper 109
Halberstam, David 168–9
Halbwach, Maurice 48
Hamas 159
Hammes, T. X. 153
    *The Sling and the Stone: On War in the
        21st Century* 153
Hapsburgs 27
Harappan civilisation 74–5
Harper, Stephen 66
Harris, Sir Arthur "Bomber" 125
Hartley, L. P. 169
Harvard Medical School 46
Harvard University 77
Hawkins, Sir John 26
Hebrew language 88, 89
Hegel, Georg Wilhelm Friedrich 15
Hello! magazine 19
Herder, Johann Gottfried 15
heroes
    current dearth of 17
    present longing for 17–18
Herzog, Ze'ev 108–9
Hindus
    lower-caste 75
    upper-caste 75, 76
Hindutva 74, 76, 77
Hiroshima, bombing of 123, 124, 135
Hispanics 120
historians
    amateur 35, 36
    Christian 39
    language 35
    liberal 124
    professional 35, 37, 39, 115

proper role for 39
self-referential historical study 35
work challenging beliefs and myths
    about the past 43–4
historic sites 4
Historica Foundation 115
Historica Minutes (Historica) 4
history
    bad 36, 37
    can be helpful, but also dangerous
        xii
    choosing to forget 113, 130
    the dustbin of (Trotsky) 9
    economic 38
    end of (Fukuyama) 10
    end of (Marx) 63
    gay and lesbian 38
    gender 38
    global 38
    helpful in self-knowledge 146–7
    Jewish 89
    as judge 20, 22
    lazy generalisations avoided by a
        knowledge of 146
    making sense of a complicated
        world 168
    one-sided or false histories xiii, 37,
        72–8
    oral 71, 105
    "patriotic" 116
    political 37, 38
    power of 8, 9, 22
    reliance on a skeptical frame of
        mind 168
    "scientific" 15
    social 38
    suppression of evidence 69–72
    treating analogies from history with
        care 157
    treating evidence seriously 167
    understanding ourselves and others
        xi–xii, 141–6
    used to label or diminish opponents
        93–6
    validation xii–xiii, 53
Hitler, Adolf 24, 37, 160
    and appeasement 159
    and Austria 134, 135
    cancels reparations burden 37
    defeat of 164
    distortion and misuse of history 100
    elevation of the nation 84
    goal of moving east 154
    murder of Jews 24
    profound German complicity 133
    and Saddam Hussein 156
    secret agreement with the Soviet
        Union 138
    seizes control of Germany 37–8
    stab in the back and unjust peace
        themes 99
    Mein Kampf 64
Hobsbawm, Eric 84
Holocaust 31, 48, 59, 96
    Chirac's admission 131
    Israel's Yad Vashem commemorates
        the Holocaust 89
    memorial in Berlin 134
    museums 4
Holocaust (American television series)
    133
Holy Roman Empire 102
Horne, Alistair: *A Savage War of Peace*
    151–2
House of Representatives (United
    States) 94
Howard, John 29, 115, 122, 136
Howard, Michael 39, 71, 142
Hull, Cordell 45, 148
human rights abuses 95
Human Rights and Equal Opportunity
    Commission (Australia) 29
Hungarians 105
Huntington, Samuel: *Who Are We?* 120
Hussein, Saddam 10, 17, 101, 145, 156,
    157, 163, 164

I
identity 53–4, 58
    American 119–20
    Israeli 109
    religious 85
    Russian 131
Illyrians 105

immigrant populations
  educating 113
  integration into the host society
    116, 119–20
  understanding British history and
    culture 117
  violence and terrorism by 114
Imperial Household Agency (Japan)
  70–71
imperialism 15–16, 66, 68, 96, 106, 121
India
  attempts to remake Indian
    education 75
  challenges United States 11
  Harappan civilization 74–5
  Hindu nationalism 73–8
  James Laine targeted 77–8
  Muslim invaders 76
Indian Council of Historical Research,
  Delhi 75
Indigenous Resistance Day (Venezuela)
  128
Indus valley 74
International Monetary Fund 148
International Olympic Committee 96
International Trade Organization 148
Internet 7, 20
internment 27–8
IRA (Irish Republican Army) 159–60
Iran 159
  Bush refuses to deal with Iran 22
  influence in the Middle East 22
Iran, Shah of (Mohammad Reza
  Pahlavi) 17
Iraq 11
  American preparation for war on
    166
  American victory over 64–5
  counterinsurgency academy in 153
  and the French-Algerian War
    151–2, 162
  invades Kuwait (1990) 10, 164
  invasion of 145, 155, 167
  Iranian influence in 22
  military failure to prepare for Iraq
    145–6
  occupation of 17, 155, 167

  oil 145
Ireland
  civil war 122
  history education 122
  major revision of its history 71–2
Irish Catholic nationalists 72
Irish potato famine 26
Islam 76
  fundamentalist 21, 158
  parallels between Iraqi and Algerian
    wars 151
Isle of Man 28
Israel
  American support for 107
  Declaration of Independence 88
  deep hostility between Palestinians
    and Israelis xii
  dispute over Palestine 105–9
  establishment of (1948) 65, 88
  German reparations to 133
  Knesset 89, 159
  and Masada 49
  military 49
  Suez crisis 160
Israel Antiquities Authority 108
Israelites 108
Italian Americans 128
Italy
  brought into being by nationalism 81
  burial of last World War I veteran 19
  claims at Paris Peace Conference
    103
  Fascist 16, 28
  led to disaster by Mussolini 62
  occupation at end of World War II
    147
  unification 61–2
Ivan the Terrible 8, 17

J
Jackson, Stonewall 57
Jacoby, Susan 165
Jamestown, Virginia: 350th anniversary
  of first settlement 56–7
Japan
  American occupation after defeat in
    1945 70

atrocities committed by Japanese soldiers 135
challenges the British Empire for hegemony 11
commemorative citizens' parade (1997) 136
drops out of League of Nations 147
illegal seizure of Japanese internees' property 24, 28
invasion of China (1937) 68, 135
Manchuria medical experiments 135
militaristic 16, 28
nationalist right and excavation of royal tomb sites 69–71
nationalists attack historians' texts on the war 135–6
occupation at end of World War II 147, 155–6
portrays itself as a victim of Nazism 135
pushed to remember recent past 132–3
rapid modernization 70
relations with China 96
and UN Security Council 96
Jericho 108
Jerusalem 108
    Holocaust museum 4
    trial of Eichmann 133
Jews
    American Jews 48
    blamed for both world wars 64
    compensation to Jewish families by German state 24
    confiscation of wealth 24
    deportation by French policemen to death camps 130
    Dispersion 88–9
    and East Germany 134
    internee "enemy aliens" 28
    Jewish history 89
    Masada story 48–9
    murdered by Ustasha 93
    re-creation of a Jewish state 48, 88
    scolded for ingratitude in criticizing Pétain 131

    Zionists 48, 88
Joffe, George 145
Johnson, Lyndon 161–2, 163
Jones, Quincy 7
Jordan 106
Joshi, Murli Manohar 75
Judaea 107

K
Karadži , Vuk 87
Kassebaum, Nancy 125
Kennedy, John F. 43, 44, 149, 150, 161, 163
    Why England Slept 161
Kennewick man 71
Keynes, John Maynard 36, 148
Khrushchev, Nikita 142–3, 149, 159
Kissinger, Henry 55, 95, 104
Kohl, Helmut 137
Korea
    enforced prostitution by Japanese 135
    influence on Japanese culture 70
Korean War (1950–53) 17, 21, 161, 162
Kosovo 48, 88, 105
Kosovo, Battle of (1389) 86–7
Kremlin, Moscow 8, 120
Ku Klux Klan 118
Kurds 90, 97
Kuwait, Iraqi invasion of (1990) 10, 101, 164

L
Labour Party 116
Ladd, Paddy 61
Laine, James 77, 78
land claims 100
Lane, Harlan 60
language classification 83
Latin American nationalists 68
Lawrence, T. E. 154–5
    Seven Pillars of Wisdom 11, 153
Laz Party 90
Lazar, Prince 86–7
Lazi 90
League of Nations 82, 147
Leftists: escaping from the present 16

Legion Magazine. "At War with the
  Museum" 126
Lenin, Vladimir 23
Leopold, King of Belgium 100
liberal capitalism 9
liberal democracy 10
liberal internationalism 11
Liddy, G. Gordon 119
Limbaugh, Rush 118–19
literacy 83
Lithuania 103
Lloyd George, David 85
Lodge, Henry Cabot 163
Longfellow, Henry Wadsworth 54, 55
Lorraine 101, 102
Los Angeles Times 119
Louis XIV, King of France 102
Louisiana Purchase (1803) 100

M
McAleese, Mary 72
MacArthur, General Douglas 17
Macmillan, Harold (later 1st Earl of
  Stickton) 42
MacMillan, Margaret: *Nixon and Mao*
  22, 67
McNamara, Robert 162
  In Retrospect 144
Maginot Line 152
Manchuria 162
  medical experiments 135
Mandela, Nelson 25
Mao Zedong 8, 17, 23, 67, 122, 143,
  156, 157, 159
Maori of New Zealand: illegal seizure
  of their land 24–5
marginalization 53
Marine Corps University, Virginia 151
Marois, Pauline 115
marriage 100
Marshall Plan 21
Martel, Charles 85
Marx, Karl 8–9, 15
Marxism 10, 63, 142
Marxist historical materialism 122
Masada story 48–9
May, Karl 55

Mazzini, Giuseppe 61–2
Mecca, Saudi Arabia 24
Meiji Restoration 70
Meir, Golda 105, 106
Memorial Day (United States) 117
memory
  collective 48, 49, 81
  recovered memories 45–6
Middle Ages 38, 39, 83, 84, 104
Middle East
  Egypt's position in 160
  Iran's influence in 22
  Jewish immigrants to Israel 88
  and Western powers 65
Miloševi , Slobodan 10, 88, 94
Ministry of Defence (British) 145
Miquelon island 100
Mitterrand, François 130, 131, 137
Monde, Le 131
Montreal, Holocaust museum 4
Moors: defeat in Spain 66
moral tales 114
Mormon genealogical records, Salt
  Lake City 7
Morris, Benny 109
Muhammad, Prophet: taking him out
  of history 24
Munich (appeasement policies in
  1930s) 158–9, 161–4
Munich conference (1938) 158–9
Museum of the Confederacy,
  Richmond, Virginia 57
museums 3–4, 5, 56, 57, 122–7, 133,
  137–8
Muslims
  and abolition of the caliphate 65
  Bosnian 87, 94
  conflicts with Christians 9
  and First World War 47–8
  fundamentalists 64
  humiliation and suffering 66
  immigrants in France 114
  in India 75, 76
  and Saudi Arabia's sacred sites 65
  and Serbs 93
Mussolini, Benito 40, 62, 84, 160
My Lai massacre (1968) 163

N

Nagasaki, bombing of 123, 135

Nanjing, Rape of (1937–8) 96, 97, 124, 135, 136

Napoleon Bonaparte 8, 38–9, 100, 129

Napoleonic Wars (1803–15) 100

Nasser, Gamal Abdel 160, 161

nation

   appearance of new nations 89–90

   celebration of achievements 81

   defined 81–2

   elevated by Hitler's and Mussolini's regimes 84

   unreal yet influential version of origins 83–4

National Air and Space Museum, Smithsonian Institution, Washington, D.C. 123–5

national archives 6

National Council for History Standards 118

National Council of Churches 128

National Council of Veteran Associations in Canada 127

National Education Goals (United States) 118

National Historic Preservation Act (1966) 5

National History Standards (United States) 119, 120, 123, 124

National Post 44

National Sorry Day (Australia) 29

national values 114

nationalism 89, 101

   ethnic 11

   German 99

   great wave of 83, 87

   history provides fuel for 81

   Hobsbawm on 84

   Indian 73–8

   Irish 122

   a late development in human history 82

   and older ways of defining oneself 82–3

   parallels between Iraqi and Algerian wars 151

Serbian 87

nationalist movements 28, 107

Nationalist Party (South Africa) 25

nationalists 58, 62

   Algerian 129

   French-Canadian xii, 68

   German 101–2

   Hindu 74–8

   Irish Catholic 72

   Japanese 135–6

   Latin American 68

   Serbian 94

Native Americans 71, 128

NATO 21

Nazism, Nazis 16, 24, 40, 60, 64, 130, 133, 134, 138, 146, 159

Negro History Week (United States) 59

Nehru, Jawaharlal 76

Nelson, Admiral Lord Horatio 151

Neustadt, Richard and May, Ernest: *Thinking in Time* 149

New Deal 38

New World 128

New York: Lower East Side tenements debate 6

New York Times 122

New Zealand: illegal seizure of Maori land 24–5

Newsweek magazine 129

Nightingale, Florence 3

Nixon, Richard 22, 67, 159

North, Oliver 119

North Africa, French colonies in 130

North Korea 158, 161

North Vietnam 144, 163, 166

Northern Ireland 146, 160

November 11 (Armistice Day) 85

Novick, Peter: *The Holocaust in American Life* 48

nuclear war, threat of 9

O

Obama, Barack 159

Ofsted 116

Old Testament 108

Olympic Games (2000) 68

Operation Desert Storm 164
Ophüls, Marcel 131
Opium Wars 68, 95
oral histories 71, 105
oralism 60, 61
Orwell, George 23
Ottoman Empire 62, 87, 102, 105
Ottoman Turks 86, 87, 97
Our Island Story 116
Oxford University 162
Oxford University Press 77, 78

P
Pacific war 135
Palestine, Palestinians xii, 88, 105, 106, 107
Palestinian National Authority 108
Pantheon, Paris 18
Paris Peace Conference (1919) 11, 101, 102–4, 105
Parris, Matthew 27
Parti Québécois 114–15
patriotism 67, 68, 117, 124
Pearl Harbor (1941) 45, 165
Pelletier, Gérard 69
Peloponnesian Wars 151
People's History, A (CBC documentary series) 4
Péronne war museum 137–8
Perth, Ontario 5
Pétain, Marshal 131
Peter the Great 3, 8, 17
Peters, Joan 106
Petraeus, General David 153
Picq, Ardant du 152
Pilgrim fathers 117
Plymouth Hoe 85
Podhoretz, Norman 158
    World War IV: The Long Struggle Against Islamofascism 158
Pol Pot 23
Poland 102, 103
    Brandt visits the Warsaw Ghetto memorial 137
    German invasion of (1939) 159
    Russian murder of Polish soldiers (1939) 138

unsuccessful invasion of Russia (1612) 131
political leaders: self-comparison to great past figures 17
politicians, lack of trust in 19
Pontecorvo, Gillo 151
Ponticelli, Lazare 18
pope, the
    apology for the Crusades 26
    and power of Roman emperors 39
Powell, General Colin 157, 163
"Preserve America" executive order (2003) 5–6
Promotion of National Unity and Reconcilation Act (1995) 25
protection 11, 148
Protestants, Ulster 72
Pune, Maharashtra
    police force 77–8
    research institute 77
Putin, Vladimir 8, 120–21

Q
Qing dynasty 104
Quebec, Canada
    French nationalists xii, 69
    history education 114–15
    motto of 114
    sympathy for the Vichy government 69
Quito, Ecuador 128

R
racism 26–7, 56, 115
Raleigh, Sir Walter 116
Rama (Hindu god) 74
Ramayana 77
Ranke, Leopold von 38
Reagan, Ronald 128, 146–7
Record, Jeffrey 164
recovered memories 45–6
Red Guards 23, 67
Reformation 58
regimental histories 54
religion
    born-again Christians 20
    evangelical churches 20

history as evidence of a divine purpose 15
moral standards and values 20
religious fundamentalism 11, 63, 64, 74, 77, 108
religious police 24
Renan, Ernest 81–2
reparations 25, 26, 37, 98, 99, 133
repentance for past wrongs 24–5
residential schools (Canada) 30–31
Revere, Paul 54–5
Reynolds, David 40
Rhineland 82, 160, 162
Richard III, King 116
Richard the Lion Heart, King 116
Richmond, Virginia 57
Right, the 157, 163
Robert the Bruce 116
Robertson, Pat 64–5
Robespierre, Maximilien de 23
Robin Hood 116
Robinson, Randall: *The Debt: What America Owes to Blacks* 30
Rockwell, Norman 16
Roman civilization 73
Roman Empire 84
Romance, Trisha 16
Romania, Romanians 104, 105
Romantics: preoccupation with the supernatural and imagination 46
Rome, ancient 73, 169
Roosevelt, Franklin Delano 20, 38, 45, 147
Roosevelt, Teddy 55
Royal Air Force 41
  Bomber Command 125, 126
Royal Ontario Museum 123
Rudd, Kevin 29–30
Rusk, Dean 162
Russia
  challenges United States 11
  collapse of 102
  desire for security 142
  Putin on the new textbooks 120–21
  relationship with China 157
Russian civil war (1917–21) 143
Russian Empire 102

Russo-Japanese War (1904–5) 152

S
St Pierre island 100
Sakharov, Andrei 132
Saladin 17
Samaria 107
Sanskrit 75
Santayana, George 147
Sarasvati 75
Sarkozy, Nicolas 100
Sartre, Jean-Paul 131
Saudi Arabia: allows American troops onto its holy land 65
Schlesinger, Arthur, Jr. 45, 117
Schroeder, Paul: 'What Has Changed Since 9/11? Not Much, and Not for the Better' 166–7
"scientific" history 15
Scotland: oil resources xii
secularism 76
segregation 56
self-determination 101, 102
Senate Foreign Affairs Committee 149
Senate Subcommittee on Veteran Affairs (Canada) 126, 127
September 11, 2001 attacks 65, 129, 145, 157, 164, 165–6
sequence 38
Serbia
  claims the Banat 104
  and Kosovo 105
  occupied in World War I 146
Serbian Academy of Sciences 87–8
Serbian army 146
Serbian Empire 86, 87
Serbian Orthodox Church 94
Serbian television 93–4
Serbs
  and Battle of Kosovo 86
  conflicts with Croats 9, 88
  history of 68
  and Kosovo 48
Shanghai, new textbooks in 121–2
sharia law 64
Sharon, Ariel 94
Shiv Sena 77

Shivaji (Hindu king and hero) 77
Shlaim, Avi 109
Sicily 83
sign language 60
Sikhs 76
Six Day War (1967) 48
slavery 31, 96, 128
    Clinton's apology 26
    and commemoration of the
      Holocaust 59
    compensation issue 30
    defenders of 169
    descendants of African slaves and
      DNA 7
    discrimination and violence after
      emancipation xii
    downplayed in textbooks 56
    Garvey on 72
    and Jamestown anniversary
      celebrations (1957) 56–7
    relationship between slaves and
      slave owners 58
Slavs 84, 93, 103
Slough, Berkshire 26
Slovenes 93
Smithsonian Institution, Washington,
    D.C. 123, 124, 125
Snow, Tony 22
socialism 65, 68
sociology 37
Socrates 73
Solomon, King 108
Somme, Battle of the (1916) 137
Sorrow and the Pity, The (documentary)
    131
Sorry Books (Australia) 29
South Africa
    apartheid 25–6, 107, 122
    history education 122
South Vietnam 144, 163
sovereignty 101
Soviet Union
    1980s admissions 138
    collapse of the Soviet Empire
      (1989) 9–10
    Communism 8, 9, 23
    Cuban crisis of 1979 149–50

    Cuban missile crisis 44
    and defeat of Hitler 164
    expansionism 17
    the Gulag 132, 138
    Hitler moves into 101
    horrors of Stalinist period 132
    huge losses in both world wars 142
    murder of Polish soldiers (1939) 138
    post-war reconstruction 142
    relationship with China 157
    secret agreement with Hitler 138
    Sino-Soviet split 143
    Truman and 21
Spain
    Law of Historical Memory (2007)
      132
    trauma of civil war and repression
      132
Spanish Armada (1588) 85
Spears, Britney 19
Stalin, Joseph
    and the Allies 16
    and Chinese Communists 143
    compares himself to previous great
      leaders 8, 17
    as a dictator 121
    and Eastern Europe 101
    ignores warnings of German
      invasion (1941) 154
    and the Korean War 161
    makes Trotsky "an un-person" 23
    motivation for moving into Eastern
      Europe 142
    revelations on the number of his
      victims 138
    and Tito 143
Stalingrad, Battle of (1943) 84
Stanley, Henry 100
Starkey, David 4
Starowicz, Mark 4
State Education Law (Israel) 89
Stephen, King of Serbia 103
"Stolen Generations" (Australia) 29, 30,
    115
Stuart, Jeb 57
subprime mortgage crisis 150
Sudan 95

Suez Canal 160
Suez crisis (1956) 42, 160–61
Summer Olympics (2008) 96
Suskind, Ron 144
Swiss banks: profits from wealth
    confiscated from Jews 24
Syria 159

T

Taiwan 95, 104
Taj Mahal, northern India 74
Taylor, A. J. P. 141
teenagers 54
television: history channels and
    documentaries 4
Tenement Museum, New York City 6
Terror, the 129
terrorism
    negotiating with terrorist
        organizations 159–60
    struggle with 21
    World Trade Center attack as an act
        of terrorism 165–6
Teutonic Knights 64
Teveth, Shabtai 109
Thanksgiving (United States) 117
Thapar, Romila 75, 77
Thatcher, Margaret, Baroness 116
Third World 160, 161
Thucydides 141
Tiananmen Square demonstrations,
    Beijing (1989) 67, 68
Tibet 95–6, 104
Tito, Marshal Josip Broz 143
Tokyo 136
Toronto terrorist plot (2006) 114
torture
    and Al Qaeda 129
    Aussaresses publicly defends its use
        129
    used in the Algerian war 129
Tours, France 85
Toynbee, Arnold 16
Trabzon, Turkey 90
trade barriers 11
Trafalgar, Battle of (1805) 85, 129
Transylvania 105

Treitschke, Heinrich von 102
Trotsky, Leon 9, 23
Trudeau, Piere 69
Truman, Harry 20–22, 161
Truth and Reconciliation Commissions
    Canada 31
    Chile 136
    South Africa 25–6, 136
Tryon, Vice Admiral George 168
Tuchman, Barbara: *The Guns of August*
    161
Tudjman, Franjo 88, 94
Turkey
    abolition of the caliphate 65
    admission to the European Union
        97
    Arab struggle against Turkey for
        independence 11
    and Armenians 97
    government interest in the
        curriculum 120
    Greco-Turkish War 62, 63
Tussauds, Madame 123

U

Ukraine 103
Ukrainians: internment of Ukrainians
    living in Canada 27–8
Ulster Protestants 72
Umatilla tribe 71
United Daughters of the Confederacy
    56
United Kingdom *see* Britain
United Nations 22, 65, 147, 164, 166
    Security Council 96
United States
    American Civil War (1861–5) xii
    American Jews 48
    apology/compensation for slavery
        30
    assimilation of new immigrants
        119–20
    attitude to Soviet Union in Cold
        War 142
    bicentennial 59
    blacks' history of slavery,
        discrimination and violence xii

capitalism 9, 38
challenges British Empire for
    hegemony 11
challenges from China, India and
    Russia 11
Constitution 119
Cuban crisis of 1979 149–50
current conditions for blacks 30
damaged by its involvement in Iraq
    11
and defeat of Hitler 164
expanding relationship with China
    157
fails to join League of Nations 147
family values 119
Gulf War 157
history education in 117–20
internees in 28
lynching in 57
myth of the American West 55–6
neoconservatives in 119, 124, 157–8
patriotic societies 117
Reconstruction era (1863–77) xii, 56
reluctance to sell China advanced
    technology 95
resentment of Southern whites
    towards Yankees xii
sale of weapons to Taiwan 95
self-perception as peace-loving
    146–7
slaves' descendants and DNA
    decoding 7
the South 56–8
and Soviet Union 21
support of Israel 107
and Vietnam 17, 121, 132, 144, 146,
    161–3
White House 144–5
United States Congress 119, 124
urbanization 83
Ustasha 93–4

V
Vajpayee, Atal Behari 78
Valour and the Horror, The (television
    series) 126
Van Gogh, Theo 114

Vance, Cyrus 150
Vanity Fair 19
Vedas 75
Venezuela 128
Venice 103
Venizélos, Eleuthérios 62
Verdun: Mitterrand/Kohl meeting
    (1984) 137
Verdun, Battle of (1916) 137, 152
Versailles, Treaty of (1919) 36, 64,
    98–100
Vichy regime 69, 130–31
Victoria (flagship) 168
Victoria, Queen 85
Vienna 134
    greets Hitler (1938) 135
    opera house 134–5
Vienna, Congress of (1814–15)
    100–101
Vietnam War (1959–75) 17, 121, 132,
    144, 146, 153, 161–3, 165, 166
Vimy Ridge, Battle of (1917) 66, 67, 85
Vimy Ridge war memorial 66
Virginia 56–8
Volkswagen car 150

W
Wall Street Journal 118
War Cabinet (British) 40
war memorials 85, 132
war on terror 66
Warsaw Ghetto 137
Washington, George 85
Washington DC: Holocaust museum 4
Washington Times, The 124
Waterloo, Battle of (1815) 38–9, 84
weapons of mass destruction issue 164
Webster, Daniel 118
West Bank 106, 107, 108
West Germany
    confrontation of its Nazi past 133–4
    pushed to remember the recent past
        132–3
    reparations to Israel 133
    two hundredth anniversary of death
        of Frederick the Great 128–9
Westminster Abbey, London 85

White, Theodore 117
Who Do You Think You Are? (television show) 7
Wieseltier, Leon 31
Will, George 124
Williamsburg, Virginia 57–8
Wilson, Woodrow 36, 98, 102
Winfrey, Oprah 7
Witzel, Michael 77
women
  perceived inferiority of 169
  rights 59
Woodson, Carter G. 59
World Bank 148
World Trade Center towers, New York, destruction of (2001) 65, 165
World Trade Organization 148
World War I xi, 66, 161
  the dead initially commemorated as fallen heroes 46
  the dead as victims of a futile struggle against Muslims 46–7
  Gallipoli landings (1915) 17
  German fighting on two fronts 154
  German surrender 98
  hideous death toll 159
  internment 27–8
  Irish nationalists fight for the British 72
  Jews blamed for 64
  post-war territorial claims 84
  posthumous pardoning of soldiers executed for cowardice 27
  Serbia occupied 146
  stalemate on the western front 36, 152

state funerals for the last veterans 18–19
World War II xi
  Allied bombing campaign against Germany 41–5
  Axis 158
  Churchill's history 39–40
  internment 28
  Japanese atrocities 4
  Jews blamed for 64
  Maginot Line 152
  official histories 40–41, 151
  proper military histories of the conflict commissioned 39
  seen as the last morally unambiguous good war 16
  and Treaty of Versailles 36
"World War III" 158, 163
"World War IV" 157–8

Y
Yad Vashem (Israel) 89
Yasukini Shrine, Tokyo 135
Year Zero concept 23
Yellow Emperor 67
Yeltsin, Boris 131
Yom Kippur War (1973) 48
Yuan Weishi 121
Yuen Foong Khong 162
Yugoslavia 10, 11, 68, 81, 87, 88, 93, 146

Z
Zhou Enlai 23, 95, 104
Zimbabwe 146
Zionism, Zionists 48, 88, 89, 105, 106